K

The Young Specialist Looks At

Pond Life

The Young Specialist Looks At

Pond-Life

WOLFGANG ENGELHARDT

Translated by Heather J. Fisher, M.A.

Edited and adapted by Roderick C. Fisher, M.A., Ph.D.
(*Lecturer in Zoology, University College, London*)

Illustrated by Irmgard Engelhardt, Claus Caspari,
Hans-Christian Friedrich and Erich Schmidt

Burke Books ▶ LONDON & TORONTO

First published in the English language April 1964
Reprinted May 1968
Reprinted January 1970
Second revised edition May 1973
© BURKE PUBLISHING COMPANY LIMITED 1964 and 1973

Translated and adapted from *Was lebt in Tümpel, Bach und Weiher?*
© Franckh'sche Verlagshandlung, W. Keller & Co., Stuttgart 1962

ACKNOWLEDGEMENT

The Publishers are grateful to S. Beaufoy, F.R.P.S., F.R.E.S.,
for permission to reproduce his photograph of an Emperor
dragon-fly, *Anax imperator*, on the cover of this book.

ISBN 0 222 00244 1 Limp
ISBN 0 222 00246 8 Library
ISBN 0 222 00245 X Paperback

BURKE PUBLISHING COMPANY LIMITED
14 JOHN STREET ★ LONDON WC1N 2EJ
BURKE PUBLISHING (CANADA) LIMITED
73 SIX POINT ROAD, TORONTO 18, ONTARIO
SET IN MONOPHOTO TIMES NEW ROMAN
MADE AND PRINTED IN GREAT BRITAIN
BY WILLIAM CLOWES & SONS, LIMITED,
LONDON, BECCLES AND COLCHESTER

Contents

5

List of Colour Plates

6

Key to Indices

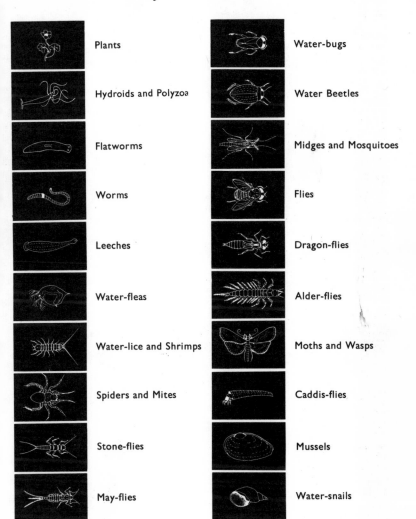

Plants

Hydroids and Polyzoa

Flatworms

Worms

Leeches

Water-fleas

Water-lice and Shrimps

Spiders and Mites

Stone-flies

May-flies

Water-bugs

Water Beetles

Midges and Mosquitoes

Flies

Dragon-flies

Alder-flies

Moths and Wasps

Caddis-flies

Mussels

Water-snails

Explanation of signs used in the illustrations:

    ♂ male

    ♀ female

    ⟨ range of actual length from ↑ to ⌉

8

Preface

In the autumn of 1953 at a conference of zoologists in Oxford a questionnaire was circulated among those attending, which asked them to state how and when their interest in biology had arisen. By far the greatest number of them said that they had been fascinated by pond-life during their school-days. The freshwater pond is in fact one of the most interesting and accessible habitats which can be explored by the young specialist who is interested in natural history. Not only are most of the major groups of animals and plants represented in the fauna and flora of ponds, lakes and streams, but they can be collected quite easily without any very elaborate equipment. Moreover, ponds and streams are common features of the countryside and even near large towns there are almost always patches of water, disused canals or flooded gravel-pits which support flourishing communities of freshwater animals and plants.

The purpose of this book is to enable the young naturalist or anyone who is interested in pond-life to identify the most important plants and invertebrate animals directly from illustrations. Obviously, only a selection from the thousands of species can be illustrated in a short book of this kind, and so all the minute one-celled animals (Protozoa) and plants (Algae), the roundworms (Nematoda), Rotifers and Gastrotricha that require the use of a microscope have been omitted. Likewise, the vertebrate (back-boned) animals, such as frogs, newts and fish, have also been omitted. Even so, it is impossible to illustrate all the species of freshwater insects, Crustacea, worms and molluscs which may be found. Accordingly, those species which you are most likely to find in each group are illustrated, together with a brief description of their characteristics and habits, which will assist identification. Even so, there are many families of invertebrate animals whose species look so much alike that they require microscopical examination for accurate identification. In these cases an animal of the most typical genus is illustrated. However, for those who wish to study any group of animals in

9

greater detail beyond the scope of this book, references are given at the end of each section to specialist keys.

Although this book is primarily concerned with the identification of freshwater invertebrate animals, a section on the vegetation of ponds and streams is included in the text. This is arranged, not according to the systematic classification of plants, but in relation to the various plant communities found in the main types of aquatic environments. Thus all the plants illustrated on one plate are commonly found together in one place—for example, a slow-flowing lowland stream. In addition to the plates and their descriptive legends, each group of animals and plants is discussed in a brief account of their structure and general natural history.

Finally, since the occurrence of plants and animals is conditioned by the characteristics of the places in which they live, an account is given of the main types of freshwater habitat and their general effects on the species of animals and plants that live in them. In this book only relatively small areas of water, such as ponds, streams and small lakes, have been considered, primarily because they can be investigated without the use of the elaborate collecting apparatus —such as boats, ropes and winches—necessary for large lakes and rivers. However, most of the species described here also occur in larger bodies of water, and the young naturalist will find this book useful for identifying animals collected along the banks of large lakes, rivers and disused canals.

Introduction

The Variety of Freshwater Habitats

All animals and plants contain in their bodies a large proportion of water, which is necessary for life. Those that live on the land have to conserve this water, as they are continuously exposed to drying out in the air. Freshwater animals and plants, however, do not need this protection, unless they live in temporary ponds and pools that dry up in hot weather; they are closely adapted to the physical features of water, which largely determine the characteristics of the aquatic environment.

Surprisingly, one of the most important features of water is that it is a liquid at normal temperatures. Apart from the metal mercury, it is the only inorganic liquid that occurs naturally in the earth's crust. It has a high latent heat of vaporisation—it vaporises only very slowly when heated; or, to put it another way, it absorbs a relatively large amount of heat for a small rise in its temperature. This means that water acts as a buffer against wide fluctuations in temperature and that large bodies of water, such as lakes and rivers, change their temperature very slowly.

All invertebrate animals are cold-blooded and cannot regulate their own body temperature. Their temperature is therefore approximately the same as their aquatic surroundings, so that in this country the animals in ponds and streams occur in greater numbers during the summer months. This is so not only because they are more active, have a shorter life-cycle and breed more quickly in warm conditions, but also because the habit that many of them have of hibernating as eggs or resistant stages in the mud at the bottom makes them difficult to find in the winter.

All animals and plants need oxygen for respiration; those that live in water breathe the oxygen that is dissolved in it. The amount of oxygen contained in natural waters varies a great deal from supersaturation in waterfalls and rocky mountain streams to almost nothing in the mud of some stagnant ponds. Freshwater animals vary in their oxygen requirements, so the amount of dissolved oxygen in the water has an important effect on their distribution.

11

Generally speaking, small animals, such as worms, flatworms and small Crustacea, have a small oxygen requirement, and can absorb all they need directly through the skin by diffusion. Larger invertebrates, such as insect larvae and molluscs, require more oxygen, and have developed special breathing organs, known as gills, for exchange of gases. Many of them have devices for the continuous circulation of water over the gills, which thus enable them to live in waters with a relatively low oxygen content. But others, such as stone-flies, have very high oxygen requirements. They are confined to fast-flowing water, where there is abundant oxygen in solution.

A few invertebrates that live in the mud of stagnant, badly oxygenated ponds have in their blood a red pigment (haemoglobin) which has a special affinity for oxygen and is capable of extracting it from the water in very low concentrations. These are the larvae of the midge *Chironomus*, a water-snail *Planorbis*, and small Annelid worms of the genus *Tubifex*. Often these are the only animals to be found living in or on the mud under very stagnant conditions.

However, many large insects, especially the water-beetles and water-bugs, which continue to live in the water as adults, have such high oxygen requirements that they cannot obtain enough from water, but have to come to the surface for air. Many of them have elaborate devices for filling their tracheal systems with air or for carrying bubbles of air down with them below the surface. These enable them to become independent of the oxygen content of the water, and so water-beetles, bugs and air-breathing fly larvae are often the characteristic inhabitants of very badly aerated waters. There are so many different adaptations for breathing in freshwater animals that they are individually discussed for each group throughout this book.

Water is also a much more buoyant medium than air in which to live. It exerts an upthrust on the bodies of all aquatic organisms, which do not therefore have to support their own weight. This enables aquatic animals to have a much more delicate structure than land-living ones. Many of these, and one-celled plants, float and drift just below the water surface in the special aquatic community known as the plankton.

Water is also remarkable for its properties as a solvent. More chemical compounds will dissolve in water than in any other liquid found in nature. About half of all the known chemical elements have been detected in natural waters, and it is likely that at least traces of all elements may occur. This means that all natural waters contain in solution some proportion of inorganic salts and other compounds, dissolved from the soil or rock on which they lie. The most abundant and important of these include carbonates, chlorides, sulphates, phosphates and nitrates. These usually occur in combination with calcium, sodium, potassium, magnesium and iron to form soluble salts. Of these, carbonates and sulphates are the most abundant salts in fresh water, while calcium, sodium and magnesium are the most important metallic radicals. Abundance of these dissolved salts in a lake produces a rich, varied vegetation and many different animal species. Such lakes, which are usually shallow and have a wide shore zone with much plant growth, are rich in basic nutrients, have neutral or slightly alkaline water and are referred to as *eutrophic lakes*.

Deep lakes, on the other hand, with little or no shallow shore zone, are poor in dissolved nutrients, such as phosphorus, nitrogen and calcium, and are known as *oligotrophic lakes*. They have little dissolved organic matter, few salts and little planktonic life.

Dystrophic lakes are usually found in boggy regions or in mountainous areas. The water in these lakes is usually dark brown in colour and has a high concentration of organic matter and humus. It is usually very acid, and often has very little dissolved oxygen. Such lakes often develop into peat bogs.

Of all these factors the three most important are probably water temperature, oxygen content and abundance of dissolved nutrient salts. Variations between them characterise a particular type of pond, stream or lake, and so determine what kinds of plants and animals can live there.

Springs and Underground Water

Springs which originate in hilly, rocky areas usually have a gravelly bottom, very clear water and no vegetation. Sometimes, however, the water wells up in a hollow forming a small, muddy pool from which a stream runs off. These usually have muddy banks and abundant vegetation. Other water sources are not so definite, and appear as seepages in banks or in marshy ground. Whatever their external features are, springs usually have cold, clear water which, like the underground water from which they run, has a steady, low temperature throughout the year. Their oxygen content is usually low and, since the water is always moving, they do not freeze in winter.

Although some springs are exceptionally rich in minerals or iron salts, which appear around their source in brightly coloured deposits, most spring water is poor in nutrients for plants. Consequently, the vegetation is usually sparse and the animals found in them are often very small in comparison with those that live in streams. They include such animals as *Crenobia alpina* and *Polycelis felina*, a few water-mites, midge and caddis-fly larvae, the snails *Limnaea truncatula* and *L. pereger* and the ubiquitous *Gammarus pulex* (Crustacea).

Underground water is very often ignored by freshwater biologists because it is usually inaccessible. Nevertheless, it exists in large quantities, sometimes in great underground rivers, especially in limestone districts. A most important feature of this underground water is that there are no green plants growing around it, because the lack of light prevents photosynthesis. But where plants cease to grow, fungi and bacteria take over. Decaying wood, old pit-props, the droppings of bats living in caves and bacteria all provide food for the curious small group of cave-dwelling animals. Most of them are worms, small Crustacea, including the amphipod *Niphargus* sp., the isopod *Asellus cavaticus* and some flatworms. Many of the underground species that live in total darkness have no body pigment, and so are completely white or colourless; they are also often completely blind. Since many of these species have closely related species living in ordinary streams, it is to be supposed that the majority of them have evolved from common ancestors, some of which must have wandered into caves and subterranean waters thousands of years ago.

Streams

The name "stream" is given to any natural watercourse up to 15 ft. wide. When wider than this, it becomes a river. Streams cannot be defined as a single habitat, because they are so variable in speed of current, structure of the bottom and watercourse, and accumulation of mud and vegetation. It is convenient to divide streams into those that are fast-flowing, with a stony, gravelly or sandy bottom (usually found in hilly districts), and those that are slow-flowing, with muddy bottoms and much vegetation (usually occurring in meadowland and lowland countryside). The fast-flowing streams have little detritus accumulation, except under stones and in occasional sandy bays, the temperature of the water is low (2–10° C.) and it is well aerated (Figure 1).

Owing to the speed of the current, both animals and plants have

Figure 1. A mountain stream (photograph: E. Bürner)

15

efficient means of clinging to the stony bottom. Higher plants are usually uncommon, and algae encrusting the stones make up most of the vegetation. Most of the animals are small and usually flattened. They crawl on the stones and have many adaptations for clinging to them. The Turbellarian flatworms crawl on the undersides of stones, as does the freshwater limpet, *Ancylastrum fluviatile*. Mites and beetles belonging to the Dryopoidea have large, clinging claws. Caddis-fly larvae attach their cases to stones as do those midge larvae that spin cases. Others have suckers, like the stream-dwelling leeches *Glossiphonia complanata* and *Erpobdella octoculata*, the black-fly larva *Simulium*, and other fly larvae.

Most of the adaptations to life in fast-flowing water are directed towards a sedentary life. This complicates the feeding processes. Some species graze on the algal covering of rocks and stones, but others have developed mechanisms for filter-feeding. Some construct nets in which they catch small animals floating in the water, as *Rhyacophila*, the net-spinning caddis, does. Others have mechanisms which enable them to filter suspended particles of food from a stream of water continuously passed through the mouth-parts.

However, the speed of water-flow in streams is very variable even within short distances, owing to the character of the bottom as well as the contour of the land over which it runs. Where the speed of the water is greatest, as in rapids or in small waterfalls, the bottom is swept clear of sediment and gravel and consists only of large stones. Few animals are found in such places. Where, however, the flow is slightly less rapid, stones and gravel collect round the larger rocks, detritus accumulates, and a larger animal and plant community is established, with stone-fly and may-fly larvae, some Turbellaria and caddis-fly larvae. Few animals live where there is only fine gravel or sand on the bottom, because of the constant movement and grinding action of the sand particles.

More usually accessible are the slow-flowing lowland streams and slow rivers (Figure 1a). These normally have more varied bottom conditions. Some parts are thickly covered with mud and decaying organic material, which provide rooting space for dense vegetation. Other stretches may be fast-flowing over gravel or sand and so have less detritus and usually less dense vegetation. The water in slow-flowing streams is usually less well oxygenated and is subject to greater temperature variations than hill and mountain streams, but their more abundant vegetation and generally less extreme conditions enable a large number of animals to live there. Also each part

16

Figure 1a. A lowland stream (photograph: R. C. Fisher)

of the stream has its own characteristics, which in effect create a microhabitat for particular organisms. Thus pond-skaters and whirligig beetles (*Gyrinus* sp.) live on the surface of calm bays and almost motionless water. Another community of animals, particularly insect larvae and snails, lives in the vegetation and water-weeds close to the banks, while a third quite different community of worms, midge and may-fly larvae and mussels burrow into the mud or live on its surface at the bottom of the stream. Each group has detritus-feeders, plant-eaters and carnivorous predators, most of which show special adaptations to the particular microhabitat in which they live.

Ponds and Small Lakes

In almost any part of the countryside and often within a short distance of most towns small areas of standing fresh water can be found. Whether they are formed naturally or by the flooding of excavations, such as gravel pits, makes little difference to the rich flora and fauna that they support. Such standing waters are usually called ponds, lakes, swamps or marshes, and since these words are

17

Figure 2. A lowland lake (photograph: W. Engelhardt)

used continuously throughout this book, some definitions are necessary.

Swamps are wet lowland areas covered with reeds, sedges and some small trees. Most of their vegetation is rooted in standing water. Marshes are generally drier, with little if any free-standing water, and are usually broad, damp areas of land covered with grasses and sedges. Ponds and lakes are more difficult to define because they originate in very different ways. However, to most people a pond is a small, quiet body of standing water with rooted water-plants growing right across it (or capable of supporting plants all the way across). Depth and light penetration are more important here than surface area, and for the purpose of this book a pond is defined as an area of standing water not more than 6 ft. deep. Many ponds are totally enclosed and are fed solely by rain-water and drainage from the surrounding land. These are some-times called "dewponds". The other type of pond is one that is created artificially by damming a stream so that the pond has both an inlet and an outlet and a slow circulation of water.

A lake, on the other hand, is any large area of standing water that occupies a land basin. It may be fed by underground springs and land drainage, but it usually has several streams or even small rivers draining into it. Deep-water lakes differ so considerably from ponds in their structure and contents that we are not concerned with them here. However, the shallow marshes of small lakes, where there is plenty of submerged vegetation, have many animals and plants in common with ponds, and they can therefore be included in this account of pond-life.

Ponds are usually surrounded by reeds and rushes and also have a dense underwater vegetation. These are of vital importance to the animal inhabitants, most of which live on vegetation in some way or another. Numerous freshwater animals crawl on plants; many lay their eggs on their leaves and stems; others eat plants or bore tunnels into them. Decaying plant material is not only an important source of food for small scavenging animals, but it provides an increasing layer of detritus and humus on the bottom. This is rapidly decomposed by bacteria in warm, shallow water, so that ammonium salts, phosphates and other nutrients are quickly released into the water for the metabolism of other organisms. Thus a shallow pond is a highly productive system which supports a great diversity of animals and plants.

During the process of photosynthesis, by which plants manufacture foodstuffs, oxygen is released, and this considerably increases the aeration of the water. A completely stagnant pond can receive most aeration of the water directly from plants in this way.

Very small ponds and flood-water pools that sometimes form in woods or in gravel pits in the spring are of special interest. Such pools have only a temporary existence when they form after flooding or heavy spring rains. They are usually completely dry by mid-summer. Nevertheless, they are often colonised by a surprising number of small freshwater animals, which are particularly resistant to the rapidly changing conditions of such places. Such animals are specially adapted to survive the drying up of the pond or puddle. They can survive for months, even years, in the dried-out mud, either as eggs or in drought-resistant cocoons. These hatch out as soon as they are wetted; within a few weeks they grow to maturity and pass through their entire life-cycle, breeding and producing resistant eggs again before the little pond dries out.

Many of these animals are the microscopic Protozoa and the Rotifers which are not covered by this book, but there are also some flatworms and several of the Crustacea, particularly the fairy

Figure 3. A pond showing an advanced hydrosere succession
(photograph: R. C. Fisher)

shrimps and water-fleas, that are found in these temporary pools. All these animals can withstand the rapid changes in temperature which occur in shallow pools and puddles, when heated by the sun. Many of the species are very rare, and the fairy shrimps in particular are inclined to turn up in a pool or large puddle for a year or two and then disappear entirely. It has been suggested that their eggs are carried from place to place on the muddy feet of water-birds, though it is likely that they are usually dispersed by the wind.

Moorland Bog-pools and Peat Cuttings

The dark brown dystrophic waters of moorland bog-pools and peat cuttings often look devoid of animal life. Little vegetation grows in these pools apart from the bog-moss (*Sphagnum* sp.), and indeed their rather unfavourable conditions make them into a special habitat in which very few animal species can live. The water is usually very acid and has very little dissolved oxygen. Most of its larger inhabitants, therefore, are insects that have special respiratory organs (dragon-fly larvae of the genera *Sympetrum*, *Libellula*, *Aeshna* and *Leucorrhinia*), or which come to the surface to breathe air, as do several species of water-beetle, especially *Dytiscus margi-*

nalis and *Acilius sulcatus*, and a number of water-bugs. Swimming in the water are fly larvae *Chaoborus*, while living at the bottom *Chironomus* midge larvae and *Tubifex* worms are common. Sometimes planktonic Crustacea are found swimming in peat cuttings, together with the water-spider *Argyroneta aquatica*.

Various features of a peat moor combine to make the peat-pool a very restricted habitat. Peat is a very bad conductor of heat, so that in shallow water the temperature changes on sunny days can be very great. There are no nutrient salts in solution, because the dense layer of impermeable peat at the bottom of the pond prevents the access of mineral salts dissolved in water underground. They are therefore fed only by salt-free rainwater.

Most important is the great acidity of the water, largely caused by the bog-moss *Sphagnum*. Most animal species and also bacteria are unable to survive in such acid water, so there is no bacterial breakdown of dead plants, and their undecomposed remains become compressed into new peat. Finally, there is very little dissolved oxygen indeed in these stagnant, weedless pools. Quite often the shallower pools have no dissolved oxygen at all below the

Figure 4. A bog-pool in a disused peat cutting (photograph: W. Engelhardt)

21

Figure 5. A disused canal (photograph: R. C. Fisher)

surface. These characteristics of moorland ponds and peat-pools.
make them a good example of the important role played by the
environment in determining the composition of the fauna.

Salt Marshes and Polluted Waters

Another example of the limiting effect of environmental factors
can be taken from pools in salt marshes or ponds heavily polluted
with sewage, where, by contrast with peat-pools, the water has too
much dissolved salt rather than too little. Animals living in these
conditions are able to survive great changes in salt concentration,
and many of them are characteristic estuarine species, like the
shrimps *Gammarus duebeni* and *G. zaddachi*. They are always found
in the varying salt concentration of brackish water, but cannot live
either in pure sea water or completely fresh water. Generally, however, salt-pools and marshes have an essentially freshwater fauna,
though leeches, mussels, snails, may-flies and dragon-flies are
noticeably absent. Midge and fly larvae, however, are especially
common.

Badly polluted waters are unfortunately very common, especially
in industrial areas. Nevertheless, there are a few species which

usually occur in vast numbers in such places, and they play an important part in purification of the water. Many Protozoa and algae are common in such places, as are many small worms, including the bloodworm *Tubifex* and *Chironomus* midge larvae and a few of the large dipteran larvae, including *Ptychoptera*, *Stratiomys* and the so-called "rat-tailed maggot", *Tubifera* (*Eristalis*).

This short summary demonstrates that freshwater habitats have considerable diversity and that each one has its own characteristic fauna and flora. It will not then be difficult for the young specialist to find at least two contrasting types of freshwater habitat not far from home, even in built-up areas or industrial districts, from which he can learn much of the lives and habits of freshwater animals and plants.

Equipment for Collecting

Fortunately, the equipment needed is simple and by no means expensive to buy. Nevertheless, you may wish to make your own.

Your pond-net must have a metal frame and be strong enough not to bend when swept quickly through the water and among water-plants. It is absolutely essential that this metal is rustless or painted with an anti-corrosive paint, otherwise it will soon rust and weaken the net around the top. Circular frames as used for butterfly-nets are not very suitable for pond collecting; when this type of net is swept across the bottom of a pond only a small part of the circumference of the net is in actual contact with the ground. A rectangular or triangular frame is much better. This shape is also useful for moving under large stones and overhanging banks.

The best length for each side of the frame is about ten inches. The net should be 12 to 15 in. deep and made of a strong material, which nevertheless allows water to pass through easily. The best materials are white nylon or cotton net with a mesh of one millimetre. Cheese-cloth, linen or calico should not be used, because they allow the water to pass out far too slowly. Jam-jars with tight-fitting, plastic, push-on caps or honey-jars with screw-on lids can be used to transport the catch.

Anybody who has specialised in a particular type of animal and collected them in large numbers at various places during his collecting tours can seldom manage without corked specimen tubes. The size of these is, of course, determined by the animal collected, but those 3 in. long and 1 in. in diameter are most useful. Nowadays it is possible to buy specimen tubes and collecting-jars made of plastic, and it is well worth spending a little money on these to save the frustration of breaking glassware while you are out collecting.

Your equipment should also include a pocket lens which magnifies ten times, a pair of forceps, a small watercolour paint-brush, an old spoon and a white enamelled pie-dish. An ordinary kitchen

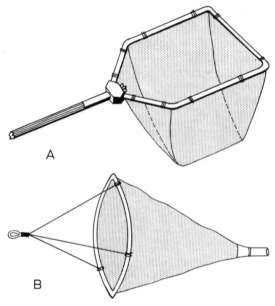

Figure 6. A. Pond-net. B. Plankton net

sieve with a wire mesh of one millimetre is useful for collecting animals that live in mud and fine gravel. For catching planktonic Crustacea, a plankton net of miller's gauze is essential, and this can be purchased at any specialist shop. You should also carry a small notebook and a pencil. Anybody who wants to study a particular group of animals or a particular type of water will not be able to manage for long without making exact notes. If a particular stretch of water is being studied closely, then all its characteristics should be entered in the notebook: e.g. the speed of the current, type of soil at the bottom, vegetation on the bank, temperature of the water, colour, etc. No useful results can be obtained by relying on memory or writing up these results when you get home. If you collect on one

24

day from several different places, then a small piece of paper with a pencilled number should be put into each jar; this number can then be placed against the appropriate entry in the notebook.

Do not be deterred by the idea that everything has already been discovered. On the contrary, apart from the largest and most common species, we have very inadequate knowledge of the types of water preferred, food, mating and life-cycle of many freshwater invertebrates. Every young specialist can do useful work here if he is prepared to record his observations accurately and conscientiously.

Before starting to collect from a pond or stream, remember that different animals live in different parts of the water. Some live on the bottom, others on the weeds, and some only under stones or in mud. Try each place in turn, and keep the animals you collect from them separately. In fast-flowing water take out a few large stones and search their undersides carefully. Many animals can be found living on branches that are lying in the water or on the sides of bridges and banks. Rich finds can be made by pulling up bunches of water-plants and sorting through them in the water-filled pie-dish. The soft larvae of stone-flies and may-flies and other soft-skinned animals are best lifted up with the paint-brush and washed into collecting-jars; larger animals can be lifted out with the spoon. In still water the net should be used to sweep along the bottom or through the water-weeds.

When taking animals home alive, remember the following points:

1. Never have too many animals in the same jar.
2. Predators should be separated and put into individual containers.
3. Empty out most of the water. The animals survive best if placed in damp moss or water-weeds which are just covered by water.
4. Make sure that there is a good air supply in each jar, and keep the animals as cool as possible by avoiding direct sunlight.

The Aquarium

Keeping freshwater invertebrates in an aquarium is not difficult, and enables you to observe much more of their habits than you can see in the pond. Those animals that live in ponds and lakes require no more than a normal still-water tank with plenty of plants rooted in sand or gravel. Species from fast-flowing water, however, must have the aquarium artificially aerated by an electric pump. These can be bought at aquarists' shops, but they are usually expensive. Details of the food required by each of the individual species will be found in the relevant chapters of this book. Water-beetles, all water-bugs, dragon-fly larvae, caddis larvae and the larger snails can easily be kept, but they must have an adequate supply of living food, e.g. mealworms and bloodworms, if they are not to attack each other. Many small larvae of insects, such as those of midges and mosquitoes, can easily be kept in jam-jars provided with a little mud on the bottom.

If you intend to start a permanent collection of a group of animals from a particular type of water, then you must make quite sure that each animal is identified and placed in a tube or jar labelled with its name and details of where and when it was found. Any further biological notes from your notebook should be entered on a card index under the appropriate species.

Preserving Your Collection

In order to make such a collection, the animals must be killed as soon as they are brought home, and then preserved in 70% alcohol. Adults of all water insects, excepting beetles and bugs, can be killed by placing them in a killing jar containing the liquid ethyl acetate, which should be dripped on to a cotton-wool pad and covered with a piece of blotting-paper. As soon as they are dead, the insects should be pinned, labelled and arranged in insect collecting-boxes.

Hydrozoa, Crustacea and the larvae of all water insects, excepting the large dragon-flies, should be killed by placing them in a glass jar containing a little clean water, to which is added a small quantity of 40% solution of formalin. After a few hours, they should be transferred to specimen tubes for permanent storage in 70% alcohol. The label should be written in pencil or in indian ink and placed inside the tube.

The large dragon-fly larvae (*Anisoptera*) and the large hard-bodied insects, such as beetles and bugs, are killed instantly if they are dropped into boiling water. After one minute they should be removed, dried and pinned. The dragon-fly larvae, however, should be preserved in 70% alcohol. Worms, flatworms and leeches must be narcotised before preserving, otherwise they contract too severely. For this purpose, they should be placed in a flat dish with very little water, to which a 5% solution of magnesium chloride should be added until they cease to move. You can also use 10%

alcohol drop by drop or crystals of menthol scattered on the water surface as a general narcotic for small fresh-water animals. Flatworms should then be placed for about twenty-four hours in a mixture of six parts of 90% alcohol, three parts 40% formalin and one part ethyl acetate, and then stored in 70% alcohol. Worms and leeches should be placed in a mixture of ninety-three parts of distilled water, two parts of concentrated nitric acid and five parts 40% formalin.

Water-mites should not be placed in alcohol or formalin, as they become too hard and contract their limbs so much that identification becomes extremely difficult. Instead, they should be preserved in a mixture of five parts of glycerine, two parts of ethyl acetate and three parts of water.

Snails and mussels should be killed in boiling water, in the same way as the dragon-fly larvae. After cooling, the soft body can be carefully drawn out of the snail shell with a piece of bent wire and can be scraped from the mussel with a blunt stick. The shells must then be allowed to dry out in the heat of a moderate oven or in the sun. If you want to preserve the whole animal, it should be kept permanently in 10% formalin.

The animals thus preserved in alcohol, formalin or other liquids should then be placed in small specimen tubes closed with wads of cotton-wool and separated according to species and origin. Tubes belonging together should then be placed in a larger, screw-capped jar, which should be filled with enough preserving fluid to cover the tubes. Owing to evaporation of the preservative, the jars must be topped up from time to time.

Plant Life

Although this book is primarily concerned with the variety of invertebrate animal life that is found in ponds and streams, one section of it must be devoted to freshwater plants. Not only do certain animals feed only on a particular species of water-plant, but, more fundamentally, the plants that live in a given type of pond reflect the geological foundation and character of the soil on which they are growing and determine the whole character of the pond environment. Hence they influence the animal fauna that can live there. For example, a shallow pond in calcareous soil (limestone or chalk) will support a large number of plant species which prefer neutral or slightly alkaline water. Their extensive growth in shallow water, owing to good light penetration, produces dense underwater vegetation, which provides food and cover for many animal species. The presence of the plants favours the accumulation of mud, silt and plant debris, which in turn favours colonisation by marsh plants, so that a reed swamp or grass marshland may develop, with its own characteristic fauna of freshwater animals.

On the other hand, a steep, rocky-shored lake in a mountain district with relatively acid water supports only a small range of plant life—partly because only a small number of plant species will tolerate acid-water conditions and partly because, on account of the steep, shelving shore, there is very little shallow water at the edge of such a lake where good light penetration allows water-plants to grow abundantly. Even when shallow acid water allows the formation of a marsh, it is quite different from the first example, and usually consists of bog-moss (*Sphagnum* sp.) and various sedges (*Carex* sp.).

As a result each type of freshwater habitat becomes clearly defined and easily recognised by its general aspect and the kind of vegetation and animal life that live there. The everyday names—pond, marsh, stream, lake, bog-pool and river—immediately bring to mind particular kinds of vegetation that are typical of each. The muddy pond has thick weeds at the edges and perhaps a fringe of reeds and water-lilies in the middle; the mountain stream with a stony bottom has little plant life in the water, but tussocky sedges overhanging its banks; the slow river with muddy water and silty bottom has a mass of vegetation at its banks and abundant submerged weeds.

These names already imply various factors which are especially important to the plants that live there. Physical differences, such as running and still water, constancy of water-level, as in a large lake, or the impermanence of temporary pools that dry up in summer, all play their parts. However, in smaller areas of water in particular, the vegetation is primarily dependent on the nutritional salt and humus content of the water. The brown colouring of peaty lakes and moorland tarns (dystrophic water) is characteristic of rich, dissolved humus material and the absence of lime and nutritional salts. The edges of such moorland lakes are fringed with characteristic bog-mosses (*Sphagnum* sp.) and sedges (*Carex* sp.).

Other types of water contain only small quantities of dissolved humus, and their waters are clear, blue, grey or green (clear-water lakes). Many of these have abundant foodstuffs and dissolved salts (eutrophic waters), thick layers of mud and silt on the bottom, masses of floating plants and a wide, fringing belt of emergent vegetation, consisting of reeds and underwater plants with floating leaves. Many mountain lakes, on the contrary, are lacking both in foodstuffs and humus and have oligotrophic waters. Although they have little vegetation by comparison with eutrophic lakes, their own restricted flora is often highly characteristic.

Plants that live wholly in water have certain characteristics that distinguish them from terrestrial ones, and each feature assists in adapting the plant to the requirements of the water in which it lives. For completely aquatic plants, the biological adaptations can be grouped under five headings.

1. In the water the plant body needs far less mechanical tissue than on the land. Most aquatic plants therefore show no sign of lignification. The buoyancy which keeps the plant upright in the water is often achieved by the formation of aerenchyma tissue. In the stems of such species, star-shaped cells are formed, and spaces between the cells are filled with air. If the plants are challenged solely mechanically—that is, not by bending, but by traction from the current of flowing water—then we find no lateral mechanical tissue, but at most a central vascular strand which supplies the necessary tensile strength. The roots, if they are present at all, serve only as anchors.

2. As water is present in excess, the regulation of the water

requirements of the plants needs little control. Often there is no extensive root system—indeed, often no roots at all. Water-carrying veins are barely developed and the surface membrane (epidermis), which otherwise hinders transpiration, and the stomata are missing (except on the upper side of floating leaves, where control of evaporation of water into the air is still important).

3. The salts dissolved in the water are not taken in through the roots, but through the whole plant, especially through the leaves. For this reason, the increase in surface area of the underwater leaves by division into fine, feathery strands, their thin texture and the lack of an epidermis are important adaptations (for the mineral salts are often only present in very small concentrations). It is perhaps significant that a few rootless plants living in waters with very low dissolved salt content increase their food supply by catching animals.

4. The plant needs not only salts, but also carbon dioxide for the process of photosynthesis of sugars. There is, of course, a quite considerable amount of carbon dioxide present in solution in water, so that the plant can absorb this important part of its food through the leaves. Whereas in land-plants the chloroplasts which contain the assimilating chlorophyll are only found on the inner layers of the leaves, in water-plants they are situated on the outer layers. A further source of carbon dioxide is calcium bicarbonate, which is often present in solution in quite considerable quantities. Carbon dioxide is absorbed by the plants, leaving a residue of calcium carbonate in the form of white chalky crusts deposited on the older leaves.

5. Much more complicated, however, are the respiratory requirements of hydrophytes, since the necessary oxygen is relatively insoluble in water. In this respect the air-storage tissue (aerenchyma), already mentioned, assists in ventilating the plant, and maintains a certain respiratory reserve.

Unfavourable conditions often deny water-plants the chance of forming flowers; their seed-production is therefore often severely hampered. This problem, however, is surmounted by vegetative reproduction. In the case of land plants, vegetative derivatives (cuttings, suckers, runners, brood-buds, etc.) must always first be firmly rooted before they can exist independently, but in water it is sufficient to have a simple offshoot which is capable of living separately. This is the only explanation of why a few water-plants, such as the Canadian Pondweed, have been able to spread over vast areas—even whole continents—although originally only plants of one sex were introduced from North America.

Water-plants cannot regularly rely on seed-production to survive the winter, since their flowers are not always developed. Many species therefore develop winter buds (turions or hibernacles) in the autumn. These take the form of short, compressed axial buds with many fleshy scales round them, which are densely packed with food reserves. These buds detach from the plant and sink to the bottom in the autumn and do not develop into new plants until the spring.

Naturally, the buds assist the dispersal of the plant over wide areas either by floating downstream with the water or by being carried in mud on the feet of water-birds. The seeds also are often well adapted for transport by water, either because of their light weight or because of special adaptations, such as inflated skins, long appendages and slime casings, which give them considerable scope for floating over vast distances. Sticky or rough fruits and seeds easily attach themselves to water-birds, and thus provide for long-distance colonisation of suitable environments. These successful methods of dispersal explain why most water-plants are widely distributed over large areas—even over two or more continents.

The Zonation of Aquatic Plants

The plants that grow in or near open water can be classified in various ways, but they are usually divided on their habits and extent of growth in relation to the water surface. Broadly, they can be divided into marsh plants (*Helophytes*) and truly aquatic plants (*Hydrophytes*). Among the latter group three broad categories are usually distinguished—"submerged", "floating leaf" and "reed-swamp"—and this division, which is roughly associated with the depth of the water, results in a zonation which can be recognised in most ponds, rivers and lakes. In addition, there is a fourth category of plants which are not rooted in the mud, but which float freely at the surface of the water or just below it.

These different life forms characterise successive stages in the "hydrosere"—the plant succession that leads from open water to reed-swamp and marshland and eventually to the complete drying up of the pond. The various stages can easily be seen in lowland ponds and small lakes in Britain, and especially in artificial lakes and waterways, such as canals which have fallen into disuse (Figures 3 and 5).

31

PLATE 1

1. White water-lily. *Nymphaea alba* L. (Nymphaeaceae.) Long, stout, creeping rhizome. Long-stalked, floating leaves. Solitary flowers, large and conspicuous, with 4 green sepals and many spirally-arranged white petals with numerous stamens; flat stigmatic discs on spherical fruit. July–August. Common in still, muddy water throughout Britain.

2. Yellow water-lily. *Nuphar lutea* (L.) Sm. (Nymphaeaceae.) Leaves more oval and with more numerous veins than in *N. alba.* Flowers with 5 striking yellow sepals and numerous much smaller petals. June–August. Common in still or slow-flowing water throughout Britain.

3. Water-crowfoot. *Ranunculus aquatilis* L. (Ranunculaceae.) Numerous, finely dissected submerged leaves on 6-ft.-long submerged stems; floating leaves rounded, palmate and 3–5 lobed. Flowers fairly large, with 5 white petals and numerous stamens. May–August. Common in still or slow-flowing water with a low lime content throughout Britain.

4. Horn-wort. *Ceratophyllum demersum* L. (Ceratophyllaceae.) Submerged aquatic herb up to 3 ft. long, with no roots and having stiff and somewhat prickly leaves in whorls of 4 branches. Flowers unisexual, inconspicuous and seldom developed; pollination occurs below water; turions. June–September. Fairly common in still, eutrophic water; rare in Wales and Scotland.

5. Spiked water-milfoil. *Myriophyllum spicatum* L. (Haloragaceae.) Sub-aquatic plant with branching shoots and 4 leaves in a whorl, pinnate and feathery. Inflorescence above the water with flowers in whorls, monoecious, inconspicuous, in the axils of smaller, almost entire bracts. June–August. Very common in still, especially calcareous water.

6. Whorled water-milfoil. *Myriophyllum verticillatum* L. (Haloragaceae.) Usually 5–6 leaves in a whorl, flowers in the axils of larger and similarly feathery and pinnate bracts. July–August. Turions. Scattered in still or slow-flowing water usually with a low lime content and abundant nutrition. Not very common in Britain.

7. *Trapa natans* L. (Hydrocaryaceae.) Annual plant with long, scaly-leaved stems and floating rosettes of leathery, diamond-shaped leaves. In the axils of the leaf stalks there are solitary, small, white, 4-petalled flowers. August–September. Not found in Britain; scattered distribution in Europe.

8. Fringed water-lily. *Nymphoides peltatum* (Gm.) O. Ktze. (Menyanthaceae.) Long, creeping rhizome, floating leaves, almost circular and like those of the water-lily, but smaller and alternate on the stems. Flowers in umbel-like panicles rising above the water, with a 5-part calyx and a golden yellow corolla with fringed edge. 5 stamens, fruit capsule ovoid, ripening under water. Reproduction usually asexual. July–August. Widely scattered in ponds and slow rivers in eastern and central England.

PLATE 1

Aquatic Plants in Still and Slow-flowing Water

The wholly aquatic plants that live in still water with eutrophic conditions form well-developed zones of vegetation fringing ponds and lakes down to a depth of about 6 ft. They may conveniently be divided into three groups:

1. Those of shallow water, which are rooted in the mud, but which have at least some of their leaves floating on or projecting above the water. Commonly, the flowers also project above the water surface, and a representative group of them is shown in Plate 1. The water-lilies, water-crowfoot (Plate 1) and arrowhead (Plate 3) are typical examples of this group. The water-lilies have stout rhizomes fixed in the mud, by means of which the plants spread vegetatively. The long leaf-stalks hold up the leaves, which lie flat on or project above the water surface. Both arrowhead (*Sagittaria sagittifolia*) and water-crowfoot (*Ranunculus aquatilis*) have differently-shaped aerial and aquatic leaves—a common characteristic of plants in this category. The submerged leaves are usually finely dissected, and have therefore a very large surface area for the absorption of water, salts and dissolved gases.

2. The second group includes those plants of deeper water which are rooted in the mud, but whose leaves are entirely submerged. Some of them project only their flower spikes above the water, such as the two milfoil species (*Myriophyllum spicatum* and *M. verticillatum*), which derive their name from the delicately pinnate feathering of their unmistakable submerged leaves (Plate 1). Others—in particular, the large family of pond-weeds, the Potamogetonaceae —live entirely submerged at the bottom of ponds and shallow pools. The leaves of these plants are usually small and very numerous, as in the curled pondweed (*Potamogeton crispus*) and *Zannichellia palustris*.

In slightly less eutrophic waters the water-violet (*Hottonia palustris*) is often found, sending its pink flowers above the surface, but often under such conditions large areas of the bottom are covered with siliceous algae, the stoneworts *Chara* and *Nitella*.

3. The plants in this group are not rooted in the mud at all, but float freely at or just below the water surface. They occur where the depth of water is so great that the leaves of rooted plants would be far too far below the surface to receive sufficient light for photosynthesis, because water absorbs light and its intensity decreases with increasing depth.

Free-floating species include the small but very abundant duck-weeds, *Lemna* sp., the fern *Salvinia natans* and the water-moss *Riccia fluitans* (No. 11). Also included are such plants as the rootless horn-wort (*Ceratophyllum demersum*), which only anchors itself tempor-arily to the bottom with its first offshoots and later lives floating below the surface. Another example is the bladderwort (*Utricularia* sp.) (No. 19), which is occasionally found in still water. It is insectivorous and has tiny bladders on its submerged leaves which trap small aquatic insects and water-fleas. Their bodies are decom-posed and absorbed, giving the plants an additional source of food. The frog-bit (*Hydrocharis morsus-ranae*) (No. 4) has a rosette of leaves that float on the water surface, with a few hanging roots, and white flowers that rise up above the surface.

A very similar community of aquatic plants to those found in ponds and lakes are those which live in slow-flowing eutrophic streams. Apart from the water movement, which tends to equalise variations in temperature, dissolved gas and salt content, similar ecological conditions prevail, which perhaps explains why the same genera occur in both places, though the species are often different. Plate 2 illustrates characteristic species, such as water-crowfoot (*Ranunculus fluitans*) and the water-moss *Fontinalis* sp. A very common plant in slow-flowing streams and canals is the Canadian pondweed (*Elodea canadensis*), a plant that was introduced from North America in about 1850 and which has since spread all over Europe.

In shallow calcareous streams, such species as brooklime (*Veronica beccabunga*) and watercress (*Nasturtium officinale*) are often so extensive as to cover the entire water surface. These species often extend into the shore flora of lakes, particularly where streams run into the lake.

Reed-swamp Plants

The reed-swamp zone of a lake hydrosere is a familiar feature of almost any lowland pond or lake. It is characterised by tall, upright plants with no branches, such as *Phragmites communis*, *Typha lati-folia* and *Scirpus lacustris*. These plants have long, creeping rhizomes which penetrate the mud in all directions and hold the plants upright. By their abundant production of buds from the rhizomes, a single species community is developed. *Scirpus lacustris* usually occurs in the deeper water on the outer fringe of a reed-swamp, and does not usually form very dense vegetation by itself. The reed *Phragmites communis* is the principal swamp-forming species. It usually lives in about three to four feet of water, although it can also live in wet mud. By abundant annual growth and deposition of its own decaying leaves and silt among its rhizomes, it can push out into the open water and so initiate the spread of reed-swamp conditions. In places such as the Norfolk Broads this type of reed-swamp can extend for miles. The reed-maces, *Typha latifolia* and *T. angustifolia* (No. 23), are often alternative dominant plants to *Phragmites* in polluted waters. The bur-reed *Sparganium* is often found in patches on the landward side of the reed-swamps in lakes and ponds, but it sometimes becomes the dominant reed-swamp plant, especially along river banks and in disused canals.

On the shoreward side of the reed-swamp and associated with it are a number of large plants, often with brightly coloured flowers. The flowering rush (*Butomus umbellatus*) and the yellow flag (*Iris pseudacorus*) are good examples, but there are many others (Plate 3), including the great spearwort (*Ranunculus lingua*) and the water-plantain (*Alisma plantago-aquatica*).

Marsh Plants

Still further from the open water and on the inner side of the reed-swamp are often large areas of damp vegetation dominated by various species of sedge (*Carex* sp.) and rushes (*Juncus* sp.). Some of these larger sedges, such as *Carex elata*, form distinct zones of their own which, although often dry in the summer months, are usually as wet as the reed-swamp in the winter. The *Carex* zone as a whole usually completes the gradation from shallow, standing water through marsh to more or less dry land. Other sedges such as the beaked sedge *C. rostrata* are found more in association with other plants, including, according to habitat, such species as the buckbean (*Menyanthes trifoliata*) (No. 29), marsh cinquefoil (*Potentilla palustris*) and the characteristic marsh plants such as marsh willow-herb (*Epilobium palustre*), water-forget-me-not (*Myosotis palustris*) brooklime (*Veronica beccabunga*), meadowsweet (*Filipendula ulmaria*) and many others.

Sometimes on the driest part of a marsh, small trees and shrubs appear eventually producing a small zone of shrubby woodland known as "carr". The principal trees are the alder (*Alnus rotundi-folia*) and various willows (*Salix* sp.) and alder buckthorns. Ideally, the carr is finally replaced by the climax vegetation of the area, usually oak forest, but this seldom occurs because agricultural land is usually cultivated up to the edge of any marshy ground. The final stage seen in most hydroseres at present is usually mixed alder and willow wood, provided that no artificial drainage of the water table occurs.

Moorland Plants

The plants numbered 31–50 are shown as examples of vegetation from waters that are naturally poor in mineral salts (oligotrophic conditions). Nos. 31 and 32 occur only in salt marshes, Nos. 33–41 are rather rare or at least local on the edges of muddy or sandy ponds in hilly or mountainous districts. All are characteristic of water that is poor in dissolved salts, and none of them occurs in calcareous regions.

The plants numbered 42–50 are typical of extreme oligotrophic water of peat cuttings and acid moorland pools, where the lack of dissolved salts is correlated with abundant dissolved humus, producing the typical brown acid water of dystrophic types. These plants, most of which have eutrophic water relatives, are chiefly found in mountainous and moorland districts.

Bog-pools, which arise by a remarkable cyclical succession of mosses and sedges on peaty moors, are often filled in with the abundant growth of species of bog moss (*Sphagnum* sp.) of which *S. cuspidatum* (No. 50) is the most completely aquatic. It is practically the only plant to grow actually in the very acid brown water, and it provides a refuge for the very few aquatic animals, mainly insects, which can live there.

Since most of the plants described here belong to a single group, the Angiospermae, there would be little point in arranging the illustrations in their respective families. Instead, they are arranged so as to illustrate a representative series of plants which you are likely to find in each ecological type of water.

For further reference:

McClintock, D., and Fitter, R. S. R. (1956). *Collins Pocket Guide to Wild Flowers*. Collins, London.

Clapham, A. R., Tutin, T. G., and Warburg, E. F. (1952). *Flora of the British Isles*. Cambridge University Press.

Keble Martin, W. (1965). *The Concise British Flora in Colour*. Ebury Press and Michael Joseph. London.

Plant Life Illustrated

See also: Plate 1, page 33

1. **Amphibious bistort.** *Polygonum amphibium* L. (Polygonaceae.) Creeping rhizome, aquatic form having floating leaves with long stems, which are leathery, smooth and elliptical; leaves of the terrestrial form have shorter stems, are thinner and have soft hairs. The leaf stalks pierce a cone-shaped stipule sheath. Flowers in a terminal cluster, pinkish red, usually dioecious. June–September. Common in still and slow-flowing canals and rivers.

2. **Broad-leaved pondweed.** *Potamogeton natans* L. (Potamogetonaceae.) Creeping rhizome, submerged leaves narrow and linear, delicate; floating leaves leathery and smooth, ovate-lanceolate, with a long sheathing scale at the bottom of the stem. Flower spike with non-thickening stem, individual flowers hermaphrodite, no perianth, 4 stamens and 4 fruits. Wind-pollinated. May–August. Very common in ponds, bog-pools or streams with shallow, acid water throughout Britain.

3. **Shining pondweed.** *Potamogeton lucens* L. (Potamogetonaceae.) Shoots up to 10 ft. long with numerous, large, elliptical, brittle and translucent submerged leaves. Stem of the flower spike clearly thickening upwards. June–August. Widespread in still and slow-flowing, base-rich water on muddy bottom in Britain, except Devon and Cornwall.

4. **Frog-bit.** *Hydrocharis morsus-ranae* L. (Hydrocharitaceae.) Floating herb with leaves grouped in rosettes, having long stems and rounded, kidney-shaped leaves, putting forth runners from the axils. Flowers monoecious, male in threes, female solitary, consisting of 3 sepals and 3 white petals, 12 stamens or 6-celled ovary with 6 bifid styles. Turions. May–August. Scattered distribution in ponds and canals, locally common.

5. **Water-soldier.** *Stratiotes aloides* L. (Hydrocharitaceae.) A free-floating plant in summer, which sinks to the bottom in winter, its leaves wide, linear, spinous-serrate and arranged in rosettes with offsets. In the leaf axils there are long-stemmed, dioecious inflorescences with flowers similar to those of frog-bit. Reproduction mainly asexual. In many places plants of only one sex are found. May–August. Scattered in ponds in calcareous districts. Very local, if not rare.

6. **Great duckweed.** *Lemna polyrrhiza* L. (Lemnaceae.) Floating plant with minute, leaf-like thalli about ½ cm. in diameter, rounded or ovate, with a tuft of roots. Rarely flowers; reproduction almost entirely asexual. Spends winter on the bottom. May–September. Widely dispersed, locally abundant in still waters in ponds and ditches, in lowland districts, cosmopolitan.

7. *Wolffia arrhiza* (L.) Wimm. (Lemnaceae.) Rootless. Thallus 1–1·5 mm.; does not flower in Britain. Rare in still water in southern England and South Wales; generally distributed in almost all subtropical regions.

8. **Duckweed, duck's-meat.** *Lemna minor* L. (Lemnaceae.) Thallus 2–3 mm., flat with only 1 root on the underside. Flowers not uncommon, June–July. Common in still water. Cosmopolitan.

9. **Ivy duckweed.** *Lemna trisulca* L. (Lemnaceae.) Partially submerged, only floating when in flower; with paired, lanceolate thalli growing at right angles, forming a cross, up to 1 cm. long with a single root on the underside. May–July. In ponds and ditches, except in south-west England.

10. *Salvinia natans* (L.) All. (Salviniaceae.) A floating fern with a stem up to 8 in. long and leaf whorls, each consisting of 2 floating leaves and one much-dissected and root-like hydrophyllum. At their base are sporocarps with macro- and micro-spores; ripe August–October. Not found in Britain; locally abundant in Germany and north-west Europe.

11. *Riccia fluitans* L. (Ricciales, Hepaticae.) Free-floating, pale-green liverwort without root hairs, up to 2 in. long, dichotomously branched. Spores only formed in terrestrial plant. Very widely distributed and often found in association with *Lemna*.

H.Or.Friedrich
del.

12. Curled pondweed. *Potamogeton crispus* L. (Potamogetonaceae.) Often reddish submerged water-plant with 4-edged stem and longish, linear leaves, finely serrated at the edges and undulate, folding round the stem. Similar to broad-leaved pondweed (No. 2). June–August. Found in still water with muddy bottom.

13. Perfoliate pondweed. *Potamogeton perfoliatus* L. (Potamogetonaceae.) Stem often branched with alternate, ovate, coarsely serrate leaves, clasping the stem. June–August. Common in still or slow-flowing water.

14. Fennel-leaved pondweed. *Potamogeton pectinatus* L. (Potamogetonaceae.) Stem much branched, thin and delicate; narrow leaves, almost string-like and mostly tapering and acute. Stipular sheath 1–2 in. long. Spike thin, about 2 in. long, with 3–4 separated flower whorls. June–September. Found in still or slow-flowing water.

15. Horned pondweed. *Zannichellia palustris* L. (Zannichelliaceae.) Submerged aquatic plant with spirally-wound rhizomes; leaves narrow and linear, up to 4 in. long, with stipular sheaths clasping the stem. Flowers monoecious, male with 1 stamen, female with perianth and 4 short-stalked ovaries. Fruit crescent-shaped, toothed along the back. May–August. Found in still, slow-flowing or brackish water.

16. *Naias marina* L. (Naiadaceae.) Annual, submerged aquatic plant with forked, prickly stem. Leaves linear, spinous-dentate, brittle, mostly in triple whorls. Flowers inconspicuous, dioecious, in axils of leaves. Underwater pollination. July–August. Found in brackish water.

17. Stonewort. *Chara aspera* (Deth.). (Charales, Chlorophyceae.) Submerged aquatic alga up to 8 in. high, with colourless threads anchored in the ground; lateral axils in whorls at nodes. Dioecious, female reproductive organs surrounded by curled, encasing threads and covered by a small "coronet"; male organs spherical. Found in calcareous, eutrophic water and often in salt water.

18. Water-violet. *Hottonia palustris* L. (Primulaceae.) Stem almost 3 ft.; pinnate, feathery leaves massed in whorls. Inflorescence springing up from top rosette of leaves with 5-part pink flowers. Fruit capsule ripening under water. May–June. Rare, in still water.

19. Great bladderwort. *Utricularia vulgaris* L. (Lentibulariaceae.) Free-floating stem bearing rows of finely dissected leaves, the tips of which form numerous bladders. Inflorescence above the water with 12 flowers; 2-lipped corolla with reflexed edges to lower lip, bright yellow. July–August. Turions. In lakes and ponds in deep water.

20. *Aldrovanda vesiculosa* L. (Droseraceae.) Free-floating, very brittle stem; densely whorled leaves; blades transformed into traps. Flowers rarely developed, terminal, 5-part, greenish white. June–August. Not found in Britain; rare in Europe.

12

14

17

19

15

16

13

18

20

H.Chr.Friedrich
del.

21. Bulrush. *Scirpus lacustris* L. (Cyperaceae.) Rhizome short. Stem up to 10 ft. high, stiffly erect, rounded and full of pulp; long leaf sheaths at the base (when found in running water, the leaves are floating, long and ligamentous). Flowers in several apparently lateral spikes, densely bunched. Individual flowers with bract, perianth of 6 bristles, 3 stamens and 1 triangular fruit. June–July. Very common in reed-swamps.

22. Reed. *Phragmites communis* Trin. (Gramineae.) Extensively-branched rhizome with numerous stalks. Stem woody, up to 14 ft. high. Leaves lanceolate, pointed, with ring of hairs at the stipular sheath (instead of a ligule). Panicle up to more than 16 in. long with spikelets of 3–8 florets and long, white-haired spike axils. Reproduction mostly vegetative. Very common everywhere in the swamps of standing and shallow water.

23. Lesser reedmace or bulrush. *Typha angustifolia* L. (Typhaceae.) Thick, creeping rhizome. Leaves narrow, about ½ in. wide, but up to 7 ft. long. Flowers monoecious; male in a small, lax upper spadix and separated from the thick, brown female spadix. Wind-pollinated. June–July. Locally common on the edge of standing or slow-flowing water in lowland regions. *T. latifolia* L., which has male and female inflorescences contiguous and broader leaves, is the more common British species.

24. Bur-reed. *Sparganium ramosum* Huds. (Sparganiaceae.) Creeping rhizome, putting out shoots with stems up to 2 ft. high. The stems are branched and bear inflorescences on the side branches. Leaves linear, keeled; flowers monoecious in dense capitula, the lower head female, the upper male. Individual flowers have 3 spathulate scales, 3 stamens or 1 ovary. Wind-pollinated. July–August. Common on muddy river banks.

25. Water-horsetail. *Equisetum fluviatile* L. (Equisetaceae.) Rhizome long and creeping; shoots up to 7 ft. high, smooth, shallowly grooved, consisting of a single segment with toothed sheaths, sometimes with lateral branches in whorls. Spore spikes terminal, blunt, consisting of many shield-shaped bracts. June–July. Not uncommon in shallow water.

26. Tufted sedge. *Carex elata* All. (Cyperaceae.) Greyish green plant growing in dense, solid parts of bogs with a sharply triangular rough stem up to 3 ft. high. Basal sheaths filamentous in decay. 1–2 terminal male and mostly 3 female spikes. Glumes blackish brown with green midrib; female flowers with 2 stigmas. Fruit unbeaked, pithy. May–June. Very common.

27. Beaked sedge. *Carex rostrata* Stokes. (Cyperaceae.) Grows in carpets, stems smooth, leaves greyish green. 2–3 terminal male and 2–3 petioled, dense flowering female spikes. Bracts reddish brown with green sepals, fruit sac spherically inflated, yellowish green. 3 stigmas abruptly drawn together into a double, toothed beak, placed horizontally. June–July. Locally abundant in wet, peaty places with standing or slow-flowing water.

28. Tufted loosestrife. *Naumburgia thyrsiflora* L. (Primulaceae.) Erect unbranched stem up to 2 ft. high, with opposite, lanceolate leaves. Dense, petioled inflorescences in the axils of the central stem leaves. Individual flowers golden yellow, 5-part, capsule spherical. June–July. Rare in marshes and shallow water at the edge of lakes and ponds in the north.

29. Buckbean. *Menyanthes trifoliata* L. (Menyanthaceaé.) Long, creeping rhizome with basal alternate, long-petioled, tripartite leaves. Terminal, dense inflorescences with 5-part flowers. Corolla petals white to pink. Stigma split in two, capsule roundish. May–July. Common on the edge of bogs and fens and small highland lakes throughout Britain.

30. Marsh cinquefoil. *Potentilla palustris* L. (Rosaceae.) Thick, creeping rhizome with several stems with feathery leaves, each with 5 or 7 leaflets coarsely serrate, often having a reddish tinge; lateral leaves blackish. Flowers in bearing umbels with 5 dark purple sepals and somewhat smaller petals, about 20 stamens and numerous carpels. May–July. Locally common on heaths and moors, usually in north England and Scotland.

22

27

21

30

29

24

26

28

25

23

H·Ch·Friedrich del.

31. *Ranunculus obtusiflorus* (Gray). Moss. (Ranunculaceae.) Stem up to 5 ft. Dissected, stiff and pointed submerged leaves; mostly 3-lobed, crenate floating leaves. Long-petioled flowers with 5 white petals, yellow at the base; stamens shorter than carpels. May–August. Found in salty and brackish water.

32. *Ruppia maritima* L. (Ruppiaceae.) Delicate subaquatic plant, rooting at the stem nodes. Leaves small and linear, with basal sheaths. Flower spikes axillary with 2 flowers; flowers have 2 stamens and 4 separated carpels. July–September. Found in salty water.

33. Mudwort. *Limosella aquatica* L. (Scrophulariaceae.) Annual plant with a rosette of linear-spathulate and entire leaves, producing runners. Solitary, pale reddish long-petioled flowers in the leaf axils. 5-part calyx and corolla. 4 stamens. June–October. Found in wet mud or where water has stood.

34. Water-purslane. *Peplis portula* L. (Lythraceae.) Annual plant with reddish, creeping stems rooting freely at the nodes. Leaves opposite, short stalks, spathulate with 2 small side leaves. Flowers axillary, inconspicuous, short-stalked mostly 6-part. Petals whitish or pink, often lacking. Fruit spherical. June–October. Found on muddy edges of ponds on lime-free ground. Scattered.

35. *Elatine hexandra* (Lap.) DC. (Elatinaceae.) Delicate annual plant, with creeping shoots rooting at nodes. Leaves opposite, short-stalked. Flowers axillary with 3 sepals, 3 reddish petals and 6 stamens. Fruit capsule roundish and trivalvular. July–September. Found in ponds or on wet mud.

36. Water-lobelia. *Lobelia dortmanna* L. (Lobeliaceae.) Perennial with submerged basal rosette of linear, stiff leaves. Almost bare stem up to 2½ ft. high. Racemes project out of the water with 5-lobed calyx and 2-lobed pale violet corolla, 5 tubular fused pollen sac, ovary 2-celled. July–August. In stony lakes and tarns with acid water.

37. Quill-wort. *Isoetes lacustre* L. (Isoetaceae.) Submerged fern; linear leaves in rosettes up to 8 in. Megaspores in leaf sheaths of outer leaves. Microspores in those of inner leaves. May–July. In lakes and tarns with few dissolved salts.

38. Shore-weed. *Littorella uniflora* (L.) Aschers. (Plantaginaceae.) Basal leaf rosette; narrow linear leaves 4 in. Male flowers in leaf axils; female flowers usually in pairs, subsessile. Corolla whitish, mostly 4-part with about 4 stamens and superior ovary. June–August. In shallow water on sandy or gravelly shores of non-calcareous lakes.

39. *Ranunculus reptans* L. (Ranunculaceae.) Grows in carpets with creeping stems rooting at the nodes. Leaves spathulate. Flowers terminal, 3–5 mm. broad, glossy yellow. Fruits oval, shortly beaked. June–August. In patches on sandy gravel; rare on lake margins.

40. Slender spike-rush. *Eleocharis acicularis* (L.) R. & Sch. (Cyperaceae.) Grows in carpets, plant up to 4 in. high, producing runners. Stem delicate with terminal inflorescences. Flowers with 2–4-bristled perianth. 3 stamens and 3 stigmas. Fruit finely grooved. August–October. In wet, sandy and muddy places on pond margins.

41. Pillwort. *Pilularia globulifera* L. (Marsiliaceae.) Fern with extensively creeping stems with rush-like leaves less than ½ in. high. Pea-sized sporocarps at leaf bases. Widely scattered on edges of lime-free, muddy ponds and lakes.

33

32

41

34

35

31

38

40

37

36

39

H.Ch.Friedrich
del.

42. Marsh St. John's wort. *Hypericum elodes* L. (Hypericaceae.) Perennial plant with fluffy hairs; stem erect and furrowed, roundish-ovate leaves wrapped round half the stem, transparent and dotted. Inflorescences with yellow 5-part flowers. June–September. Scattered at the edge of ponds and pools on acid soil.

43. Floating scirpus. *Eleogiton fluitans* (L.). (Cyperaceae.) A perennial with creeping or floating stems bearing leaves and branched near the top. Leaves very narrow, spikes long-petioled, round, greenish. 3–5 flowers bare with blunt bracts, 3 stamens, 3 stigmas. July–October. Widely distributed.

44. Small bur-reed. *Sparganium minimum* (Hart.) Fr. (Sparganiaceae.) Leaves 2–20 in. long, 2–8 mm. wide, flat on both sides, erect or usually floating in water. Each flower-head in the axil of a tall leaf. June–August. Scattered in ditches and ponds on acid ground. Widely distributed.

45. Intermediate bladderwort. *Utricularia intermedia* Hayne. (Lentibulariaceae.) Rootless plant, anchored by means of shoots. Bladders only on the colourless stems. Green stems with extensively dissected leaves. Rarely produces flowers; pale yellow. July–September. Very local in shallow, peaty water.

46. Long-leaved sundew. *Drosera intermedia* Dreves & Hayne. (Droseraceae.) Perennial plant with basal rosette of blunt, obovate leaves with short, white glands on the upper surface and on the edge long red tentacles. Insectivorous. White 5-part flowers in cymes on curved, erect scapes, 5 stamens, superior 1-celled ovary. June–August. Locally common in damp, peaty places on heaths and moors, occasionally in *Sphagnum* bogs.

47. Marsh clubmoss. *Lycopodium inundatum* L. (Lycopodiaceae.) Sterile shoots up to 8 in. long, creeping, held by many roots, with many, awl-shaped leaves. Fertile branches erect, up to 4 in. high, with sessile cones and, in the axils of small bracts, sporophylls. June–September. Rare or local on wet lowland heaths.

48. *Scheuchzeria palustris* L. (Scheuchzeriaceae.) Perennial plant with slightly branched stems up to 8 in. high with two rows of leaves, which are grooved, dark green and basally sheathed. Flowers in poor, lax racemes with 6 greenish perianth segments, 6 stamens and 3 carpels. June–August. Very rare in wet *Sphagnum* bogs.

49. Mud-sedge. *Carex limosa* L. (Cyperaceae.) Stem producing runners up to 16 in. high, three-cornered, rough at the top and with sheaths at the base. Leaves narrow, mostly folded. Male spike terminal, thin, the 1–2 female spikes petioled, thicker and pendant. May–June. Locally common in very wet bogs.

50. *Sphagnum cuspidatum* Ehrh. (Sphagnaceae.) Dark to light green moss with long, pointed stem leaves and mostly sickle-shaped curved branches. Branch leaves lanceolate, often curled at the edges. Spore capsules at the tip of very shortened lateral branches, spherical. Scattered and common in boggy moorland.

49

42

48

43

44

45

46

50

47

H. Ch. Friedrich
del.

PLATE 2

1. Water-crowfoot. *Ranunculus fluitans* Lam. (Ranunculaceae.) Submerged, round stem up to 20 ft. Leaves (lower ones having long stems and upper leaves sessile) in very long, firm, pointed segments. Flowers up to 1 in., with 5–10 white petals, numerous stamens and small simple fruits. June–August. Found in fast rivers and streams with stony bottoms.

2. Canadian pondweed. *Elodea canadensis* Michx. (Hydrocharitaceae.) Submerged aquatic plant with branched stems up to 10 ft. Leaves longish and finely serrulate, 3 in a whorl. Female flowers rarely developed, no male flowers. Reproduction vegetative. Common in slow-flowing waterways.

3. Water-moss. *Fontinalis antipyretica* L. (Bryophyta, Fontinalaceae.) Bushy submerged aquatic moss. Stem up to 20 in. with triseriate, small, acutely-keeled leaves. Spore capsules of the dioecious plants almost sunk into short lateral shoots. Common in springs and streams.

4. Brooklime. *Veronica beccabunga* L. (Scrophulariaceae.) Creeping rhizome, stems round with leaves opposite, somewhat fleshy and oval. Flowers in loose axillary racemes with 4 sepals and 4 azure blue petals; 2 stamens, ripe capsule heart-shaped. May–September. Common in calcareous streams and marshes.

5. Narrow-leaved water-parsnip. *Berula erecta* (Huds.). (Umbelliferae.) Half-submerged with thin rhizome and hollow stems up to 3 ft. Leaves alternate, simply pinnate, irregularly serrate. Flowers in umbels with 10–20 rays. July–September. Found in ponds, streams and marshes.

6. Starwort. *Callitriche verna* L. (Callitrichaceae.) Perennial, aquatic or subaquatic plant with floating leaves; stems up to 14 in. Lowest leaves linear; floating leaves set in a rosette, spathulate. Flowers in leaf axils, insignificant, monosexual and monoecious. Fruit, small, oval, keeled. April–October. Found in ditches, ponds and fast streams or on wet mud.

7. Watercress. *Nasturtium officinale* R. Br. (Cruciferae.) Stem round and hollow up to 24 in.; leaves alternate, pinnate, the lower ones with long stalks, 1–3 leaflets, the upper with 5–9 leaflets, lobed; bitter taste. Flowers small, white, up to 50 in 1 inflorescence, each with 4 sepals and 4 petals, 2 shorter and 4 longer stamens. May–October. Common in clear, cool, flowing water.

8. Large bitter-cress. *Cardamine amara* L. (Cruciferae.) Angled stems full of pulp. Leaves with short stalks, 5–11 leaflets, crenate; bitter taste. Flowers larger than in watercress, in groups of up to 20. Anthers purple. Found in springs and on wet ground and peat.

9. *Montia lamprosperma* Chamisso. (Portulacaceae.) Mostly perennial, delicate plant, growing in a thick carpet; stem up to 1 ft., prostrate, with opposite, spathulate leaves. Flowers solitary or in small axillary cymes, 2 sepals, 5 white petals, 3 stamens. Fruit single with shiny black seed. May–October. Found on wet ground and stream banks.

PLATE 2

PLATE 3

PLATE 3

1. Sweet flag. *Acorus calamus* L. (Araceae.) Stout, creeping rhizome. Leaves ensiform, reddish at bottom and undulate at edge. Spadix up to 3½ in. long, surrounded by long sheath. Individual flowers inconspicuous, hermaphrodite, 6 segments. Reproduction vegetative. May–July. Introduced. Local in shallow water at edges of ponds.

2. Water-plantain. *Alisma plantago-aquatica* L. (Alismataceae.) Rhizome knotty and thickened; leaves in basal rosettes, the first ligamentous, later leaves long-petioled, ovate to lanceolate. Branched inflorescence with white or pink flowers; 3 sepals, 3 petals, 6 stamens and about 15–30 simple fruits. June–August. Found in shallow water with muddy bottom.

3. Arrow-head. *Sagittaria sagittifolia* L. (Alismataceae.) Perennial plant, over-wintering by means of turions borne at ends of slender runners. First leaves linear, later long-petioled, sagittate and towering out of the water. Flower stalk triangular with flowers in whorls, lower ones female, upper male; latter tripartite, white with many stamens. June–August. Found in shallow water or still or slow-flowing muddy water.

4. Flowering rush. *Butomus umbellatus* L. (Butomaceae.) Rhizome short; basal rosette of long, twisted, 3-edged leaves up to 3 ft. long. Umbel leafless with 15–50 reddish white flowers; 3 sepals, 3 petals, 9 stamens and 6 carpels each. June–August. Common locally on muddy banks of ditches and canals.

5. Yellow flag. *Iris pseudacorus* L. (Iridaceae.) Strong rhizome with sword-shaped leaves. Stem bearing several yellow flowers, each consisting of 3 outer, curved, perianth segments with dark markings and 3 inner upright and smaller segments, 3 stamens and basal 3-part ovary. May–June. Common in marshes, swamps, woods and in shallow water at edges of ponds and rivers.

6. Great spearwort. *Ranunculus lingua* L. (Ranunculaceae.) Perennial with stem up to 5 ft. high; small, lanceolate and entire leaves. Flowers 1–1½ in. in size, golden yellow with 5 sepals, 5 petals, numerous stamens. June–August. A local plant of marshes and fens.

7. Mare's-tail. *Hippuris vulgaris* L. (Hippuridaceae.) Creeping rhizome with shoots up to 3 ft. long, unbranched, hollow and towering out of the water. Leaves in whorls of 6–12, linear. Flowers inconspicuous and single in leaf axils without sheath (with only 1 stamen sessile on the basal ovary). June–July. Abundant in lakes, ponds and slow streams with high lime content.

8. Fine-leaved water-dropwort. *Oenanthe aquatica* L. (Umbelliferae.) Half-submerged, with stems up to 7 ft. high, hollow and grooved. Submerged leaves (if present) finely dissected; aerial leaves 3-pinnate with ovate lobes. Flowers in umbels with 8–12 rays, white. Usually no sheath, small awl-shaped leaves. June–September. Found in shallow or stagnant water on a muddy bottom.

Animal Life

Sponges (*Porifera*)

The freshwater sponges all belong to one family of siliceous sponges, Spongillidae, most of which are found in the sea. When fully grown, they are incapable of any movement, and live in still or slow-flowing water attached to stones, mussel shells, leaves or plant stems. In lakes they are often found at considerable depths, but they are not found in shallow pools. These animals do not have a specific individual shape; the same species can differ widely, according to environment.

Generally they take the form of flat, knobby encrustations, although long, finger-shaped projections are sometimes developed in still water. They are yellowish-white to brownish-red in colour, but when in a bright light they often appear greenish, owing to the presence of single-celled algae (*Pleurococci*), which live in the sponge. A somewhat unpleasant iodine-like smell is very characteristic of the living sponge. On the body itself an outer skin can be distinguished, which surrounds the main inner mass of the soft body like a roof, supported by spicules of silica, which form the skeleton.

Figure 7. Gemmules of the freshwater sponge
(*Euspongilla lacustris*)

The surface of the sponge is covered with numerous irregular small pores from which fine interconnecting canals lead into larger tubes that join up with adjacent tubes and finally culminate in a hole on the surface (*osculum*), which is clearly visible with the naked eye. The *oscula* each possess a collar cell with a lashlike appendage (*flagellum*), which beats rhythmically, driving a continuous stream of water through the canal system of the body of the sponge. Minute food particles and dissolved oxygen, as well as the silica for building the spicules, are extracted from this stream of water. At the same time waste materials are carried out with it. Foodstuffs pass from the flagellated cells to movable, wandering cells (*amoebocytes*) in which digestion takes place.

Sponges have no nerve fibres or sense organs. The sexes are separate, but male and female sponges cannot be distinguished by their external features. A spherical ciliated larva develops from the fertilised egg and swims about freely for twelve hours, and then attaches itself to some object. By autumn it has grown into a small sponge from 3 to 20 mm. in diameter. It then passes the unfavourable weather conditions of the winter months in the form of a gemmule (Figure 7).

While the remaining sponge tissue dies away, *amoebocytes* group together at several points into dense masses. These are surrounded by a wall, which consists of one or two layers of chitin and a layer of spicules, like a sac. In the spring they creep out again and within a few days grow to form a new sponge body.

For further reference see:
Stephens, J. (1920). The Freshwater Sponges of Ireland, *Proc. Roy. Irish Acad.*, **35**, 205.

Hydroids (*Coelenterata*)

Like the sponges, the Coelenterates of our inland waters are derived from marine forms. There are two principal genera, *Hydra* and *Cordylophora*. They prefer water which has abundant vegetation, but they can be found both in still and flowing water. They usually attach themselves to water-plants by the base of the sac-like body, while the other end, with its mouth opening, surrounded by from four to twenty tentacles, projects freely into the water. Particularly characteristic are the stinging cells (*cnidoblasts*), which are found in large groups on the tentacles and in lesser numbers over the rest of the body. They are used to catch prey and as a means of defence, and also as an aid in movement.

There are four types of cnidoblasts. The penetrants have a thread with three sharp barbs at the lower end and three rows of smaller spines. They puncture the skin of the prey so that the irritating and paralysing fluid contained in the hollow cavity of the cell can penetrate into its tissue. The smooth threads of the volvants ensnare the bristles and legs of the prey, while the glutinants, of which there are two forms of differing size, enable the animal's own tentacles to hold on to plants, etc., during movement. Although they do not swim, Hydras are very mobile, and can move from place to place either by looping or by turning somersaults. They are very greedy, and when hungry seize any prey which comes into the range of their tentacles, even if it is considerably larger than themselves. Among their prey are principally small Crustacea, worms, insect larvae and water-mites. Digestion takes place partly by the secretion of enzymes in the body cavity and partly in the body cells themselves. Indigestible residues are pushed out through the mouth. Hydras can go without food for a considerable period of time.

Reproduction is usually by means of buds which develop in the body walls and later separate off. At certain times of the year, however, they reproduce sexually. The sperm cells develop in small bulges just below the ring of tentacles, while the eggs develop similarly, but nearer the base of the body. The sperm cells are discharged into the water and swim to the eggs. Small, complete Hydras hatch from the fertilised eggs. The capacity for regeneration of the freshwater Coelenterates is quite incredible. Even particles of one-fifth the diameter of the original animal can develop again into complete Hydras.

Cordylophora lacustris originally inhabited the sea, where its related forms, the Clavidae, still occur. It is certain that this

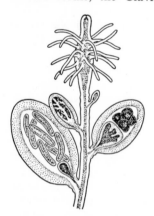

Figure 8. Part of a colony of *Cordylophora lacustris*; one feeding polyp and four reproductive polyps (× 15)

Coelenterate has comparatively recently made its way into fresh water, and is only common in certain estuaries on the East Coast of Britain. Whereas in *Hydra* the buds separate off from the mother animal, in *Cordylophora* they remain permanently attached to their parent. Thus extensively branched colonies are built up, attached to the substratum by a blackish root-like structure. The individual polyp is club-shaped and has the mouth opening on a small cone. At the lower end of the cone there is a ring of more than twenty tentacles.

Cordylophora has separate sexes, and there are therefore male and female colonies. During reproduction pear-shaped blisters, in which the sex cells are formed, develop below the nutritive polyp (Figure 8). A ciliated larva (*planula*) develops from the fertilised egg, and swims freely for twenty-four hours before attaching itself and growing to form a new colony. Only the root survives the winter, as the branches of the colony die off.

Moss Animalcules (*Polyzoa*)

By far the greatest proportion of moss animalcules live in the sea. Only about ten freshwater species are known in Europe. They are found in all types of water and only appear to avoid water with a particularly high lime content. They live in large colonies, which differ greatly in size and shape. They can have finely-branched tendrils or spherical clumps only a few centimetres in diameter. In each individual it is possible to distinguish the soft body consisting mainly of the gut and its housing, in which it is secured by means of a *funiculus*. In some species the housing consists of dark brown chitin, while in others it is yellowish white and jelly-like.

The most beautiful and striking organ of the moss animalcules is their crown of tentacles. These are arranged in numerous double rows on a circular or horseshoe-shaped supporting organ. When at rest, this projects out of the opening in the housing and can bend in any direction. If danger approaches, it can be retracted by means of strong muscles (Figure 9). By means of continuous, co-ordinated beating movements, the tentacles suck in food, such as diatoms, the smallest planktonic animals and detritus.

The Polyzoa are hermaphrodite. The sperm cells are usually formed on the funiculus and the eggs are formed on the inside of the housing wall. In most of our native species the egg is fertilised within the body cavity, and then develops in a special egg chamber to a whitish ciliated larva. When it has developed to about 1–2 mm. in size, the larva breaks out and swims around freely in the water for a few hours. Then it attaches itself, usually not far from the parent colony. The ciliated covering then opens and the first two individuals of the new colony emerge.

Further growth occurs by means of buds, which lead a regular type of branching formation characteristic of the species. In autumn a third form of reproduction can be observed, when *statoblasts*

Figure 9. Individual animals of a Polyzoan colony

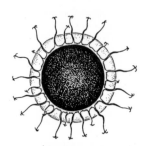

Figure 10. Statoblast of *Cristatella mucedo* (× 50)

form on the funiculus. These dark brown, oval or spherical capsules consist of two hard, horny shells which enclose cell tissue capable of germinating. Many statoblasts have a ring of cells containing air, making it possible for them to rise to the surface of the water (Figure 11). Others have spines with which they attach themselves to some object (Figure 10). In the spring the shells open and the young colony creeps out.

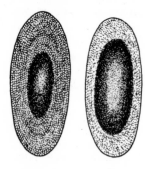

Figure 11. Statoblasts of *Plumatella fruticosa* (× 40)

Flatworms (*Platyhelminthes*)

The free-living flatworms (*Turbellaria*) are characterised by minute hairs, or *cilia*, which cover the whole of their bodies. These enable the animal to move and also create currents of fresh water for respiration. Individuals can swim freely in the water when small, while the more mature ones glide like snails over stones and weeds, often leaving a slime trail. In the skin of almost all Turbellarians there are numerous small, dark, rod-like bodies called "rhabdites", which can be expelled into the water. They are used as a means of attack and defence, for enveloping their prey in slime and for the creation of a protective casing in the event of severe drought. Two orders of ciliated flatworms occur in Britain, the Rhabdocoela and the Tricladida.

The Rhabdocoeles have a simple sac-like gut and, usually, two eyes. The shape of the body is always flat dorso-ventrally, but can be leaf- or ribbon-like in outline, according to species. Colouring and markings also differ greatly and are often determined by symbiotic algae. Most species are carnivorous; all are hermaphrodite. The young animals (after self-fertilisation) normally produce several generations of young, which develop quickly and then bore their way out through the body wall of the parent. The parent animal suffers no damage, and as soon as it is fully mature it produces thick-shelled eggs which remain inside the body and only become free when it dies. The Rhabdocoeles prefer warm, stagnant water with ample vegetation and are principally found in the summer months. There are about ten British genera and they are all very small.

The Triclad Turbellarians are usually larger in size. They are flat, mostly dark grey, brown, black or dirty white in colour. Their gut is divided into three branches, which in turn have many side branches, which may join with one another. They feed largely on living or dead animals, which are sought out with the aid of two olfactory organs (ciliated grooves) situated near the head. The prey is then surrounded by slime from the rhabdites and the pharynx is protruded, allowing digestive secretions to emerge. The tissues of the prey thus dissolved are then sucked up. When necessary these worms can survive for months or even years without food. They are hermaphrodite, and when mating occurs each partner functions as both male and female. The eggs are laid in groups in cocoons, and they escape from the parent by bursting the body wall. In many species these hard-shelled, dark-coloured cocoons are simply dropped into the water. In others they are attached by threads to stones, water-plants, etc. (Figure 12). Development is direct and there are no larval stages. Reproduction by splitting in two is also common. Their powers of regeneration are extraordinarily well developed; even the thousandth part of an animal can grow to a full-sized individual.

Figure 12. Egg cocoon of *Dugesia lugubris* (× 10)

Triclads prefer cool, running water (springs, streams and the edges of lakes). They generally avoid the light and are thus chiefly found on the undersides of stones, dead branches and floating leaves of water-plants. There are twelve or thirteen British species, six of which are illustrated in Nos. 57–64.

For further reference see:

Reynoldson, T. B. (1967). A Key to the British Species of Freshwater Triclads, *Freshwater Biological Association Scientific Publication No. 23.*

Reynoldson, T. B. (1958). The Quantitative Ecology of Lake-dwelling Triclads, *Oikos (Acta Oecologica Scand.)*, **9**, 24.

Hairworms (*Nematomorpha*)

Hitherto only five species of hairworms have been recognised in Europe. These all belong to the genus *Gordius* and are difficult to distinguish. They are found in ponds and lakes as well as in pools and flowing water. The animals are of separate sexes, and for reproduction the males and females often group together in clumps. Each female lays several thousand eggs grouped together in long strings of whitish masses of spawn. From these hatch small larvae with boring apparatus at the head consisting of three sharp prongs with a crown of spines. They bore their way into water-insects or may even be swallowed by them. In their specific hosts—for example, the *Dytiscus* beetle larvae or dragon-fly nymphs—they develop to full size in about six weeks. They then leave the host, which they have by then almost entirely consumed, except for the gut and the tracheal system.

True Worms (*Annelida*)

(i) FRESHWATER WORMS WITH BRISTLES (*Oligochaeta*)

Most species of the Oligochaeta, to which the well-known garden worm belongs, live on land; a smaller number live in fresh water and some in the sea. In the terrestrial and freshwater forms it is very difficult to distinguish between species, especially when they live in mud. The completely transparent species found in fresh water are generally smaller than the related terrestrial species. Some build themselves tubes in the mud, on stones or on water-plants, while others move by creeping or swimming. They feed on decayed remains of plants, small invertebrates and algae. All species are hermaphrodite. When mating, the two partners lie back to front and bring their sex organs, in the front half of the body, close together. Under the protection of a thick covering of slime expelled from the sex segment, the sperm is exchanged. The eggs are laid in groups in cocoons, which first of all encircle the body of the worm like a belt and the ends of which close up when the worms creep backwards out of them after mating.

The cocoons, which are varied in shape and often transparent, have chitinous walls. They are found on the bottom of ponds or on water-plants. Development is direct. The regenerative powers of worms are great and many of them reproduce asexually by budding. In this event, a division zone forms between two body segments. The front half develops a new posterior end, while the back half develops a new head. This process can be repeated several times by some species before the newly formed animals separate. As a result chains of individuals can be temporarily developed.

For further reference see:

Cernosvitov, L. (1945). Oligochaeta from Windermere and the Lake District, *Proc. Zool. Soc.*, **114**, 523.

Brinkhurst, R. O. (1963). A Guide to the Identification of British Aquatic Oligochaeta, *Freshwater Biological Association Scientific Publication No. 22.*

(ii) LEECHES (*Hirudinea*)

There are thirteen species of leeches in the fresh waters of Britain. They live in lakes, ponds, streams and ditches. They normally only avoid rapidly flowing and moorland water and prefer shallow water with abundant vegetation. They rarely penetrate below a depth of 2 ft., but avoid the light by resting beneath stones, in the crevices of submerged branches and among leaves. Owing to their well-developed body muscles, all leeches are exceptionally mobile. In locomotion the front sucker is detached and the head stretches forwards. Then the front sucker clings fast to the surface, the hind one lets go and the body is drawn up into a hump, bringing the hind sucker up to a position just behind the front one. The process is then repeated. The fish leech (*Piscicola*), the horse leech (*Haemopis*) and the medical leech (*Hirudo*) are also able to swim.

All leeches feed solely on animal matter. There are, however, two distinct groups: the *Erpobdellidae* and *Haemopis* are carnivores and they devour all sorts of smaller animals or tear out pieces of them; the rest suck blood from their hosts, which are usually amphibians or water-birds. The gut of these blood-suckers has numerous blind sacs for storing the blood, and also contains micro-organisms which help to break down the blood for food. When leeches are fully fed they can survive up to a whole year without feeding again. Respiration is through the skin. They also cast off the cuticle frequently, sometimes daily, particularly after feeding abundantly or when in stagnant water with a poor oxygen supply.

Figure 13. Cocoon of *Erpobdella octoculata* with young about to hatch (× 6)

All our native leeches are hermaphrodite. They sometimes mate in pairs, but self-fertilisation also occurs. The eggs are laid in cocoons (Figure 13). In the family *Glossiphonidae* the adult takes care of the young, but the method varies markedly from species to species. Many attach the egg capsule to water-plants. The mother then sits above them with the body humped up, and from time to time makes special respiratory movements to supply the eggs with

Figure 14. Position of eyes (left to right): *Piscicola geometra; Hemiclepsis marginata; Haementeria costata; Glossiphonia complanata; Glossiphonia heteroclita; Helobdella stagnalis; Hirudo medicinalis; Erpobdella octoculata*

well-oxygenated water. In other species—for example, *Helobdella stagnalis*—the eggs are attached to the underneath of the parent and carried around until they hatch. The young then remain for several weeks clinging fast to the abdomen of the parent. In this species and in *Glossiphonia heteroclita* the suckers of the young animals have protrusions which fit exactly the skin papillae of the mother and make it possible for the young to attach themselves very firmly. Leeches are often carried into different waters while clinging to floating wood, or to water-plants, as well as when attached to the body of their host.

For further reference see:
Mann, K. H., and Watson, E. V. (1954). A Key to the British Freshwater Leeches, *Fresh-water Biological Association Scientific Publication No. 14.*

Arthropods
CRUSTACEA
(i) FAIRY SHRIMPS (*Euphyllopoda*)

The very primitive crustaceans known as the "fairy shrimps" live exclusively in fresh water from the Arctic to the tropics. Some are found in salt marshes and lakes, but never in the sea. In Britain there are three species of fairy shrimps, only one of which is likely to be found. They are widely dispersed, and at the same time very rare. All inhabit shallow pools, which dry up after a short time. Two orders can be distinguished from the type of body covering: the Anostraca have no shell (carapace), while the Notostraca have a large carapace which covers most of the body.

The Anostraca swim with their ventral side uppermost. Their eleven pairs of flat, leaf-shaped limbs serve not only as swimming legs, but also as gills for respiration and as filters for straining out food particles (detritus and algae) and leading them to the mouth. The Notostraca can swim either way up and can also creep along the muddy bottom. Often they lie almost buried in the mud. Their chief means of locomotion is the first pair of legs, which have long bristles. They are carnivorous and live mostly on larvae of aquatic insects and worms.

In the Anostraca males and females occur almost in equal numbers; in the Notostraca males are often not found for several years, and so reproduction usually takes place without sexual union. The eggs of all the fairy shrimps have highly resistant shells, and they can survive months of drought or freezing. In many species this is essential for the development of the eggs. They are carried around for days or weeks by the female in a special brood-container and then ejected into the mud. *Nauplius* larvae hatch from the eggs, which develop quickly and breed as soon as they reach sexual maturity.

(ii) WATER-FLEAS (*Cladocera*)

These small crustaceans inhabit all still fresh water, from pools to lakes. However, individual species require quite specific habitats and are characteristic of them. The greatest number of species is found among the weeds at the edges of ponds and lakes, but vast numbers of individuals, often of a single species, are free-swimming in the plankton. They swim by making jerky movements of the two large, double-branched antennae. The thoracic legs are used almost entirely for collecting food. The slim legs of the predatory water-fleas, e.g. *Polyphemus pediculus*, are armed with bristles, with which they catch smaller water-fleas and Copepoda, which are then torn up by the jaws.

In the majority of our water-fleas the thoracic limbs are leaf-like, flattened and covered with a comb-like fringe of hairs; with the ventral parts of the thorax, the carapace and the abdomen, they form a filter system which extracts food, such as algae, bacteria and detritus, from the water and passes it to the mouth. Special appendages on the limbs are used for breathing. In addition, exchange of gases takes place through all thin-skinned parts of the body and through the walls of the rectum, which, when not discharging faeces, is rhythmically pumped full of water and emptied again.

Water-fleas lay two kinds of eggs. In one species only females are produced for several generations, and they produce unfertilised eggs. These virgin or "summer" eggs have thin shells and little yolk. From the oviduct they enter the brood pouch, which in many species is a sac-like pouch on the abdomen and in others is simply the space between the abdomen and the carapace. Here the summer eggs develop very quickly—often within two days—into small but complete miniatures of the adults. They leave the mother through a split in the walls of the brood pouch or through the space between the carapace and abdomen. They are usually sexually mature after three moults. The number of unfertilised eggs in each brood varies according to the species, age and food available to the animals. In the case of *Daphnia pulex*, for example, it is forty or more.

Towards the end of summer the unfertilised females begin to lay other types of eggs. Males hatch from some of these. Others are resistant eggs requiring fertilisation by these males if they are to develop. These resistant or "winter" eggs have a large quantity of yolk and are always surrounded by a tough, many-layered shell. After fertilisation they only pass through a few stages of development in the brood pouch; then they lie dormant for several days, weeks or months, according to the time of year, and can survive drought and frost in this state. They do, however, remain dormant, even though conditions are favourable. The predaceous water-fleas release these resistant eggs directly into the water. Other species form an ephippium, which is a saddle-shaped case providing special protection for the resistant eggs (Figure 15). Only females

Figure 15. Resistant egg (ephippium) of *Daphnia pulex* (× 20)

hatch from these eggs, producing further generations of females by the development of unfertilised eggs. Most water-fleas survive the winter as dormant eggs. The number of generations resulting from reproduction without sexual union (parthenogenesis) as well as from sexual reproduction during the year varies according to the species and is determined partly by heredity and partly by environment. Dormant eggs or those in an ephippium naturally increase the likelihood of water-birds carrying them from place to place.

For further reference see:

Scourfield, D. J., and Harding, J. P. (1958). A Key to the British Species of Fresh-water Cladocera, *Fresh-water Biological Association Scientific Publication No. 5*, 2nd Edition.

(iii) *Copepoda*

In European fresh water only three sub-orders (Calanoidea, Cyclopoidea, Harpacticoidea), with a few dozen species, are known. In addition, there are several very different parasitic forms, living mainly on fish, which will not be considered in this book. Wherever water-fleas are found there are sure to be Copepoda as well, but they are also often found with Ostracoda in water-holes formed in hollow tree stumps and similar small patches of water. Three different groups can be distinguished according to general habitat, movement and feeding habits which largely correspond to the three sub-orders.

The best-known native representative of the Calanoidea is the genus *Diaptomus*. It swims rather jerkily by beating the very long first antennae. Copepods can also glide through the water in shallow, horizontal curves, using the second pair of antennae and the feelers which are attached to the jaws. They live in the clear-water zone of lakes and ponds. As true "filter-feeders", they use their densely bristled mouth-parts to sieve their food, such as tiny planktonic organisms and diatoms, out of the water. In doing this their mouth-parts beat backwards and forwards about 1,000 times per minute, setting up whirlpools of water, which continually.bring in fresh water with more food in suspension.

The Cyclopoidea are true "swimmers", and they are found in the plankton or among the plants on the edges of still water. The Harpacticoidea, however, with the main genus *Canthocamptus*, live chiefly on the muddy bottom. The last two groups feed on already decomposing organic material. In mating, the male clings to the female and deposits a spermatophore (capsule containing the sperm cells) on her abdomen. The eggs are fertilised as they emerge from the oviduct and are carried around for a short time by the female in an egg-sac of hardened slime. The Copepoda produce both quick-developing eggs and resistant eggs, which have first to undergo a resting phase, during which they can survive drought. The Cyclopoidea and the Harpacticoidea can secrete a slime coating through special glands if unfavourable conditions occur. Using this together with particles of mud, they build a cyst in which they can survive long periods of frost or drought. This enables them to inhabit small temporary areas of water. Free-swimming larvae, known as *nauplii*, hatch from the eggs. At first they have only three pairs of limbs, the first and second antennae and the mandibles. In the course of several moults—up to twelve have been counted—which depend largely on the water temperature, the remaining limbs are added and the final body form attained.

For further reference see:

Gurney, R. (1931). *British Freshwater Copepoda*, Vols. I, II, III. Ray Society, London.

Harding, J. P., and Smith, W. A. (1960). A Key to the British Freshwater Cyclopoid and Calanoid Copepods, *Freshwater Biological Association Scientific Publication No. 18*.

(iv) *Ostracoda*

There are about 230 species of Ostracoda that live in the fresh waters of Britain and north-west Europe. There is hardly a single type of water in which these minute crustaceans with a mussel-like, double-valved shell are not found. The majority of species are found in ponds with plenty of vegetation, but certain species are characteristic of particular kinds of water, such as pools, springs and underground or cave water.

Most Ostracods live on the bottom, where they crawl along in the surface mud or in the tangle of plants. Those that climb have spinning glands on the second antennae secreting a substance which enables them to cling to smooth leaves. Other species burrow through the mud, and many can swim quite well, at least for short distances. Both pairs of antennae are used in swimming. The first pair beats swiftly backwards, while the second pair moves inwards towards the abdomen and backwards; the two contrasting movements provide sufficient power to drive the animal forwards in a straight line. Their principal food consists of decomposing leaves and dead animals.

Very little is known of the reproduction of Ostracods. In many species both sexes occur; others reproduce parthenogenetically. The eggs, which have a double shell, go through a resting period before hatching. The newly hatched larvae have a double-valved shell, but only three of the seven pairs of adult limbs. They moult several times as they increase in size before achieving sexual maturity. The resistance of these crustaceans to desiccation is remarkable. In many species not only the eggs, but also the larvae and adult animals, can survive drought for exceptionally long periods when their water habitat dries up or freezes. Some species only occur as adults in the spring, others solely in the summer, while yet others are found the whole year round.

(v) WATER-LICE (*Isopoda*)

Numerous species of water-lice live in the sea and on land, but only one genus, *Asellus*, is a true inhabitant of fresh water and only three species have so far been recorded in Britain. *Asellus aquaticus* and *A. meridianus* have no particular requirements for their habitat. It should merely not have any forceful current and must contain decomposing matter, which they feed on. Where these requirements are fulfilled, they are often found creeping on the bottom or slowly climbing up water-plants. They can, however, swim quite skilfully. When mating, the male, which is considerably larger, settles on the back of the female for about a week. During actual copulation the two partners lie with ventral sides together.

Females carrying young can be found at all times of the year. Their four front pairs of thoracic legs have curved side lamellae (or scales) which partially overlap, and thus create a sealed-off space under the abdomen. The eggs are laid in this brood-sac; on hatching, the young are carried in it until they are complete miniatures of the adults. Three to six weeks are necessary for this development, according to the temperature of the water. Usually a female lays about fifty eggs. Damaged legs or antennae are commonly cast off by the water-lice and regenerated in a very short time.

(vi) FRESHWATER SHRIMPS (*Amphipoda*)

The most important family is the *Gammaridae*, with the main genus *Gammarus*. Freshwater shrimps inhabit almost all types of water having abundant dissolved oxygen and a high lime content. They are rarely found below a depth of 6 ft. They are commonly found under stones, but are very active. The bodies of Gammaridae are laterally compressed and they usually swim on their sides. Their main food consists of living and decomposing plants, detritus and dead animals. Before mating, the larger male clasps the back of the female for about a week. The female has wide lamellae on both sides of the second and fourth thoracic segments; these lean together and form an open-ended tube along the ventral surface. In this the eggs are laid and fertilised.

The number of eggs varies from twenty to over 1,000, according to age, food supply and the conditions in which the animal lives. On hatching from the eggs, the young are already almost fully developed. They moult about ten times until they achieve full maturity—during the summer every five to seven days and in winter much less often. Reproduction takes place throughout the year. In summer, development of the young takes from two to three weeks and in winter it lasts longer. In favourable water they often develop in masses: more than 400 in 1 sq. m. have been counted. They provide a major source of food for trout.

For further reference see:

Reid, D. M. (1944). Gammaridae (Amphipoda), with a Key to the Families of British Gammaridae. *Linnean Soc. of London, Synopses of the British Fauna*, **3**.

(vii) CRAYFISH (*Decapoda*)

The Decapoda comprise the familiar lobsters, shrimps and crabs of the seashore. The only regularly found species in British fresh waters is the river crayfish, *Astacus pallipes*, belonging to the sub-order Astacura, although several other species have been introduced from the Continent from time to time. The handsome species illustrated in Plate 4 is *Astacus leptodactylus*, an Asian species that just extends into western Europe, but not into Britain.

The British species *A. pallipes* is much smaller, about 10 cm. long, and has relatively smooth pincers and cephalothorax. It is generally a greenish-brown colour and is found in streams, lakes and rivers of medium or high calcium content. It is absent from soft water. Its actual distribution in a suitable river, however, is not determined by the speed of the current, but by the presence of suitable hiding-places—for example, underneath river banks, beneath stones or in sunken tins. As nocturnal creatures, they like to spend the day in such hiding-places. Usually they crawl slowly along the bottom, using the second to fourth thoracic pairs of limbs. If disturbed, they swim jerkily backwards by flicking the tail fan and abdomen powerfully forwards under the body. They are scavengers and feed principally at night on worms, water-insects, snails, mussels and any decaying animal material. The prey is seized with the large pincers of the first pair of thoracic limbs and broken up with the smaller pincers of the second and third pairs, and finally led to the mouth-parts by the three pairs of maxillipeds.

Normally, the crayfish mates in late October and November. When mating, the male clasps the female with the large pincers and throws her forcefully on to her back. Then, using the tube-shaped first two pairs of abdominal limbs, which are modified for the purpose, he deposits sperm-masses on the abdomen and tail fan of the female. The fertilised eggs adhere to the abdominal segments and are carried around on them for six months. In the following May or June the young hatch. Their thorax is distended spherically and the abdomen is very thin, but in general they resemble the adults. Up until the first moult, on about the tenth day, they continue to cling to the abdomen of the mother with their pincers. The number of eggs varies from ten to several hundred, according to species and the age of the animal, but seldom more than a third of them reach maturity. The crayfish moults repeatedly as it grows until it attains sexual maturity in its fourth year; thereafter it moults only once a year. When moulting, a diagonal split first appears between the cephalothorax and the abdomen. The shell of each of these two sections of the body is cast off whole and later consumed. The hardening of the new body covering takes about a week. During

69

this time the soft-skinned crayfish is particularly vulnerable; it does not eat and never voluntarily leaves its hiding-place.

For further reference see:

Hynes, H. B. N., Macan, T. T., and Williams, W. D. (1960). A Key to the British Species of Crustacea: Malacostraca, *Fresh-water Biological Association Scientific Publication No. 19.*

ARACHNIDA
WATER-SPIDER (*Argyroneta aquatica*)

Although several species live in damp places near water, *Argyroneta* is the only species that spends its whole life submerged. It occurs in still water of various types, but it principally prefers moorland ponds, peat cuttings and ditches. During the warmer times of the year it often stretches its abdomen out above the surface of the water to obtain fresh air for its tracheal system. With its silk, it spins bell-like nets under the water, which are normally fixed to water-plants and filled with air. The air is collected from the surface as single bubbles, which coat the abdomen of the animal and gleam like silver. In order to do this, the spider stretches only the tip of the abdomen with the spinnerets above the surface and separates a small volume of air with its fourth pair of legs, which are held bent diagonally across the back and abdomen. When the animal dives from the surface, the air bubble is carried down with it. There are various types of bells. Those most commonly found are feeding and summer shelters, in which the spider lives and eats its prey and in which mating takes place.

The food of the water-spider varies according to its age, and consists of small Crustacea, water-lice and larvae of various water-insects. The prey is usually carried into the shelter, and there covered with an albumen-like secretion from the digestive glands before it is ingested. For moulting, which occurs repeatedly during its life, the spider usually constructs especially thick moulting shelters. When ready for mating, the males spin small sperm shelters, which have a spun band at their centre running diagonally to their longitudinal axis. On this band the male sets the seminal fluid; he then takes it up with his palps and goes in search of the female.

After mating in her living shelter, the female normally spins an egg shelter, which is usually situated just below the water surface. It is divided into two chambers. In the upper she lays the eggs, twenty to 100 in number; she herself occupies the lower chamber, watching her brood, camouflaging the egg shelter with algae and providing it with fresh air. The eggs are laid at the height of summer and the young hatch after two to three weeks, remaining for about a month in their nursery. It is not known how they feed during this time. Special shelters are not always spun; in many instances the water-spiders make use of natural hollows of a suitable size in the walls of the bank or in tree trunks, etc., which are then fitted out with a web. Winter is spent partly in the water and partly in specially constructed winter shelters, although the younger animals often spend the winter in the empty shells of water-snails. These are fitted out with webs by the spiders and filled with air, so that they rise to the surface and can there be frozen in without harm to the occupant.

WATER-MITES (*Hydracarina*)

The water-mites have evolved from terrestrial forms, and most of them (more than thirty families, with numerous species) live in fresh water. With the exception of very dirty water, puddles which dry out and surf regions without plant life, they can be found almost anywhere. Many species can be regarded as characteristic forms for certain types of water. The adults are easily recognised by their unsegmented body and four pairs of legs. These legs often show modifications which are adapted to their habitats. Those water-mites which inhabit streams usually have large claws and stiff bristles for clinging on; the legs of those which swim freely in still water are at least partly covered with a thick fringe of fine swimming hairs; those which live on the bottom have legs typically formed for creeping.

All water-mites are predators. Their prey consists chiefly of small Crustacea of very varied types (Ostracoda, water-fleas, Copepoda) and soft-skinned larvae of water-insects, such as gnats and may-flies. These are seized with the palps, pierced with the mandibles and sucked. Only the liquid contents of the prey are consumed, and the empty skin is discarded. The water-mites have a tracheal system of finely-branched tubes, which bring oxygen to all their organs. Two breathing holes (spiracles) which are situated on the mouth-parts lead into two air chambers, into which the main tracheal trunks open up. The spiracles are closed with a thin membrane, through which the oxygen is absorbed from the water into the respiratory system. The water-mites therefore do not come to the surface to breathe.

The females lay their eggs either singly or in groups on water-plants or stones. The number of these red, brownish or yellow eggs varies between one and 1,000. In development, the young mite usually passes through six stages before reaching maturity. In the egg a second egg-shell is usually formed beneath the original shell, and within this the embryo develops. The larva hatching from this shell represents the first larval stage, which has only three pairs of legs. It must now seek out a suitable host on whose blood it can feed. The larvae of many species come to the surface of the water and there attack pond-skaters and mosquitoes. Others cling to the larvae or pupa of mosquitoes, may-flies, dragon-flies, etc., and undergo the change from larva to the mature adult with their host. Others suck blood from insects which live entirely in the water, e.g. water-beetles or water-bugs.

In some mites the parasitic stage is completely lacking. Normally, however, the small parasite retracts its legs and grows into an immobile sac-like form, which is the first pupal stage (third stage). From this emerges (as the fourth stage) the second larval stage, which resembles the adult entirely, except for the immature sex organs. It also has four pairs of legs and swims freely for a time before changing into an immobile second pupal stage again. From this the sexually mature animal finally emerges. The duration of each stage varies considerably in different species. Both larval and adult forms have been observed as hibernating forms.

For further reference see:

Hopkins, C. L. (1961). A Key to the Water-mites (*Hydracarina*) of the Flatford Area. *Field Studies*, Vol. 1, No. 3.

Soar, C. D., and Williamson, W. *The British Hydracarina*, Vols. 1–3 (1925, 1927, 1929). Ray Society, London.

INSECTA
STONE-FLIES (*Plecoptera*)

The stone-flies are highly characteristic freshwater insects; all their larvae, with only a few exceptions, live in flowing water. Stone-fly larvae, which are superficially very like those of may-flies, can readily be distinguished from them because they have three segmented tarsi, each with two claws and only two cerci at the end of the abdomen. The may-fly larvae have three caudal tails and one segmented tarsus each, with one claw. The stone-flies' preference for rapid, clear and unpolluted streams is explained by their high consumption of oxygen. They are generally found on the underside of stones or in dense masses of water-plants, where they creep around slowly. Only rarely do they swim, and when doing so their legs act as oars and the abdomen assists by moving from side to side.

The larvae of the smaller species (e.g. *Nemoura*) live on green algae and diatoms as well as on various soft or decomposing plant residues. The average-size creatures (e.g. *Chloroperla*) eat small animals and plant residues equally well. The large species (e.g.

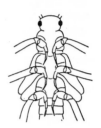

Figure 16. Ventral view of the thorax of *Taeniopteryx* sp., showing gills on the coxae

Perla) are voracious invertebrate carnivores and take rotifers, small Crustacea, worms and insect larvae. In seeking prey, the large-faceted eyes are less important than the long, slim, jointed antennae, which have numerous tactile hairs and bristles, as well as remarkable spikelets, which may be organs of taste or smell. The smaller species breathe only through their cuticle, but the larger species have string-like tracheal gills. These are simple or branched, and are situated in bunches on various parts of the body, according to the genus, either on the side walls of the thoracic segments, between the tails or on the first segments of the leg (coxae).

Figure 17. Ventral view of the pro-thorax of *Amphinemura* sp. with tufted gills

Figure 18. Ventral view of the pro-thorax of *Protonemura* sp. with tufted gills

The duration of development has only been measured for a few species. In general, the small forms take about a year from egg to winged insect; the average ones take one and a half years and the large species take from two to three years. The larvae are very similar to the adults, especially when they approach maturity, and they

73

have large, dark wing outgrowths. They clamber up on to the bank for metamorphosis. The cuticle splits along the back of the thorax and then gradually the thorax, head and abdomen are drawn out from the larval skin. There is therefore no pupal stage.

The adults have reduced mouth-parts and take hardly any solid food. During their life of four to six weeks, they live on the store of fat which they built up in their bodies as larvae. They prefer dark hiding-places on the underside of leaves, in the cracks of tree bark or under bridges. They do not fly well and rarely venture far from water. When mating, the male sits beside the female and clasps one side of her back. After fertilisation, the female carries her eggs for some time, compressed together into a ball with a sticky secretion, on the underside of her abdomen. Then she lays them in the water. To do this she creeps along the bank and dips her abdomen below the surface. A female can produce from a few hundred to about 2,000 eggs.

For further reference see:

Hynes, H. B. N. (1958). A Key to the Adults and Nymphs of the British Stone-flies (Plecoptera), *Fresh-water Biological Association Scientific Publication No. 17.*

Kimmins, D. E. (1950). *Plecoptera. Handbook for the Identification of British Insects.* Royal Entomological Society, London.

MAY-FLIES (*Ephemeroptera*)

Like the stone-flies, adult may-flies are only found near fresh water, in which their larvae live and for which they have evolved many special adaptations. The burrowing types (*Ephemera* sp.) live in slow-flowing water with muddy banks and bottom as well as close to the banks of large lakes. Their dagger-like upper jaws serve as burrowing instruments and the flattened forelegs act like shovels. In still water with abundant vegetation the swimming may-flies, such as *Cloëon*, are found. When at rest they cling to the leaves of water-plants. Many species of this group can take in water through the anus (like dragon-fly larvae) and suddenly eject it, so that the animal is thrust forward by the jet. Fast-flowing streams are inhabited by such genera as *Ecdyonurus*, whose flattened bodies are perfect examples of the adaptation to the environment. These larvae avoid the light and cling to the underside of stones. They can run fast sideways like crabs and never swim voluntarily. Creeping larval forms are found on the bottom of very varied types of water. They

74

are covered with a dense coating of hairs, in which so much mud settles that they cannot often be seen.

Most may-flies feed on the coating of algae on stones and water-plants as well as on organic mud particles. They breathe through thin-skinned tracheal gills, which are situated on both sides of the abdomen and vary in shape according to the species. The youngest larvae do not have gills, and respire through the cuticle. The mature larvae can be distinguished by their blackish-brown wing out-growths, which reach to the first abdominal segment. The cuticle of

Figure 19. Ventral view of *Rhithrogena* sp., showing the enlarged first pair of gills

the winged insect develops under the cuticle of the last larval stage. Air gradually collects between the two layers of cuticle, eventually causing the animal to rise to the surface like a cork. Metamorphosis almost always occurs in the evening and usually takes place at the water surface, although some species climb on to vegetation before completing their transformation. The cuticle splits along predetermined lines.

The whole metamorphosis from larva to fully winged adult lasts only a few seconds, a minute at the most. The animal hatching from the larval shell is, however, not yet a fully mature adult insect, but an intermediate stage, or sub-imago, which must moult once more before the animal achieves sexual maturity. This stage may last from a few minutes to about thirty hours, according to the species. The sexually mature may-flies usually live only a few hours, two to three days at the most; more rarely, but only in the case of the females, they live from two to three weeks. Their legs are so weak that they can only be used for sitting, but not for walking, while the degenerate mouth-parts do not permit them to feed.

During the day the insects lie hidden; it is not until a few hours before sunset that mating occurs. The males often form large swarms and fly up and down, usually at the same spot. As soon as a female flies into the swarm, several males pounce on her. The quickest one, hanging upside-down, clasps her thorax with his long forelegs, while his wings lie folded back beneath her. Mating is com-

75

pleted before the pair reach the ground. The partners immediately separate. The male dies shortly afterwards and the female usually starts egg-laying immediately. The females of many species fly close over the surface of the water, dipping their abdomens into the water from time to time to lay an egg. Others, whose larvae inhabit fast-flowing streams, creep down water-plants or stones and attach their eggs below the surface of the water. The number of eggs laid by the female varies from several hundred to a few thousand, according to the species. The larval stage lasts one year in most species.

For further reference see:

Macan, T. T. (1961). A Key to the Nymphs of the British Species of Ephemeroptera, *Freshwater Biological Association Scientific Publication No. 20.*

Kimmins, D. E. (1972). A Revised Key to the Adults of the British Species of Ephemeroptera, *Freshwater Biological Association Scientific Publication No. 15.* 2nd revised edition.

WATER-BUGS (*Hemiptera–Heteroptera*)

The name "water-bug" is not a systematic term; it embraces a number of bug families which are more or less adapted to an aquatic life. They can, however, be easily recognised, for they all have piercing mouth-parts, formed into a rostrum or kind of snout, with which they suck their prey; their front wings are sclerotised, or hardened, at the base, while their distal part is membranous, and they have incomplete metamorphosis. We can distinguish two groups to which several families belong. The pond-skaters live almost exclusively on the surface of the water and spend the winter in hiding-places on dry land. The water-scorpions, water-boatmen and the lesser water-boatmen undergo their complete life-cycle from egg to mature insect in the water. The families differ so greatly in their habits that we shall deal with each separately.

(i) POND-SKATERS (*Gerridae*)

The pond-skater *Gerris* lives chiefly on the surface of still or slow-flowing water. By using the surface tension of the water, the pond-skaters skim over the surface, but can also jump considerable distances. They are kept dry by a thick pile of hairs which hold air and which are particularly dense on the underside of the body. They feed principally on dead or dying insects which have fallen on to the surface of the water. The males are smaller than the females and are often carried around for days on the backs of the females. The breeding habits of many species have not yet been studied in detail. As far as we know, the eggs are attached in rows just below the water surface to parts of plants. The female *Gerris najas*, with the male on her back and surrounded by a bubble of air, submerges for up to thirty minutes under water.

Five larval stages have been observed. Many species have only one, others two generations in a year. In western Europe the one genus, *Gerris*, has ten species. Within a single species some individuals are found with normal wings, others with short wings and some completely wingless, so that it is often difficult to distinguish adults from nymphs.

(ii) WATER-GNATS OR WATER-MEASURERS (*Hydrometridae*)

The two species of the water-gnat live close to the banks and among the plants at the edge of stagnant or slow-flowing water. In contrast to the *Gerridae*, they move very slowly and have their bodies clearly raised up from the water surface. Their prey consists of water-insects which rise to the surface to take air as well as those which drift on the surface. Mating occurs throughout the early summer. A female lays eggs several times during the season and attaches them individually to water-plants or vegetation on the banks. There are five larval stages and usually two generations in a year. The adults spend the winter on the bank under stones, etc. In both species there are long- and short-winged adults as well as wingless forms.

(iii) WATER-CRICKETS (*Veliidae*)

Bays in the banks of streams and rivers are the favourite habitat of both native species of the water-cricket. There they run skilfully over the surface of the water even against the current, but they can also dive below the surface. Their prey consists of all sorts of animals which are carried along by the water. Mating occurs in the spring. The eggs are probably laid on plants on the bank. Five larval stages have been counted. There is only one generation a year. Even in winter these animals can be observed running on open water. Both species have wingless as well as winged forms. This is also true of the three species of *Microvelia*. These minute pond-skaters live together among the plants at the edges of ponds and feed on small insects which have died and fallen on to the water. The eggs are laid in long rows on floating plants. Five larval stages and two or three generations a year have been observed.

(iv) *Mesoveliidæ*

This family is represented in Britain by only one species (*Mesovelia furcata*), which chiefly lives along the banks of ponds, where it creeps on the floating leaves of water-plants or on the surface of the water. Mating occurs in early summer. The eggs are injected into water-plants a few millimetres below the water surface. Five larval stages have been observed and there is only one generation each year. The adults spend the winter on the bank under plants or as eggs. Both wingless and long-winged adults can occur.

(v) *Hebridae*

The insects in this family are very small. The only two British species (*Hebrus pusillus* and *H. ruficeps*) live in *Sphagnum* moss, but also crawl on the open water surface of moorland ponds. They suck the sap from plants. Mating occurs in May. There are five larval stages and one generation each year. Little is known of their egg-laying habits. The adults spend the winter in the *Sphagnum* moss.

(vi) WATER-SCORPIONS (*Nepidae*)

Both the water-scorpion, *Nepa cinerea*, and the water stick insect, *Ranatra linearis*, prefer still or slow-flowing water as their habitat. *Nepa* stays close to the banks, while *Ranatra* ventures further but rarely beyond the plant line. Usually they sit motionless on water-plants or on the bottom. They often go so deep that only the long breathing tubes extending from the abdomen reach up to the surface. In this position they lie in wait for their prey, which consists of small water-animals of all kinds. In doing this, the forelegs are extended forwards so that the first segment and the elongated foot form an obtuse angle. If the prey comes within their reach, the foot claps back like the blade of a knife on to the first leg segment; the prey which has thus been secured is then drawn up to the head and probed with the rostrum.

Mating occurs in spring. The relatively large eggs are provided with string-like breathing tubes (six to eight in the case of *Nepa* and two in the case of *Ranatra*). *Nepa* lays her eggs in soft or decomposing plant residues or in masses of algae, etc. *Ranatra* bores them in rows into plant stems. The young larvae hatch in May to July, and then develop through five moults to the mature insect by September. The breathing tubes of the larvae are very short and only reach their final length at the last moult. Both species spend the winter as adults.

(vii) *Naucoridae*

The common *Ilyocoris cimicoides* lives in still water where there is abundant vegetation and no current. The dense hair covering of the underside of the body and the back of the abdomen holds a gleaming air bubble which supplies the tracheal system. Its powerful hind legs, covered with swimming hairs, make it a fine swimmer. The strong forelegs are used to seize prey—water-animals of all types up to the size of young fish. Its bite can be quite painful to man. During mating in April and May the male sits on the back of the female. The female embeds her eggs (by use of the ovipositor) in plants below the water surface. The larvae hatch after a few weeks and pass through five moults. The adults spend the winter in water with abundant vegetation.

(viii) *Aphelocheiridae*

There is only one British species, *Aphelocheirus montadoni* Horv., which lives mainly in flowing water with a stony or sandy bottom. Adults and larvae live on the bottom, where they run about and sometimes bury themselves to a depth of several decimetres. They never come to the surface for air, but absorb oxygen from the water by remarkably adapted spiracles. The animals suck water-insects and mussels of *Sphaerium* sp. The eggs are laid on mussels or branches, etc. Both larvae and adults can be found throughout the year. Five larval stages have been established.

(ix) WATER-BOATMEN (*Notonectidae*)

The water-boatmen are widely distributed throughout Britain, and there are four species. They live in the upper layers of standing water. Most characteristic of them is their habit of swimming upside-down. On the ventral surface there are four thick, longitudinal rows of black hairs, which lean together in pairs, thus forming two canals. As these are filled with air, the centre of gravity of the body shifts towards the back and so the animal turns on its back. Normally the insects hang at rest just below the surface of the water, using as supports the claws on their fore and middle legs as well as the stiff hair bristles which stand out from the edges of the last abdominal segment.

Air is taken in through the two spiracles at the end of the body. After it has passed through the tracheal system of the body, it passes out through the other abdominal spiracles into the hair channels already described. The water-boatmen feed on various water-animals, especially water-insects and fish eggs. They use their hind legs as their main swimming organs, and these are fringed with long swimming hairs. The bite of the water-boatmen can be quite painful to man and can lead to local inflammation.

The eggs are attached to water-plants or buried in plant tissue. Some species lay them in the spring and they spend the winter as adults; others lay first in the autumn and the young spend the winter in the egg stage. The larvae closely resemble the adults and undergo five moults. *Notonecta* can fly well and in the autumn often seeks water which has abundant vegetation and oxygen.

Closely related is the smaller *Plea leachi* MacGreg, which is said to feed principally on water-fleas. After mating in June, the female buries the eggs in plants. The larvae which hatch in mid-summer moult five times and then spend the winter as adults.

(x) LESSER WATER-BOATMEN (*Corixidae*)

The thirty-two species of the lesser water-boatmen live commonly in large swarms in water of all types, including brackish or salt water. As their body is surrounded by a thin layer of air, which is held on the abdominal side by fine hairs and on the back by the wings, the animals are lighter than the water. They must therefore cling to the bottom or to water-plants with their claws if they are not to float to the surface like corks. As most of the air is kept beneath the wings, the position of the body is normal, i.e. back uppermost. To take air in, they thrust the head and thorax out of the water at brief intervals, when air is probably absorbed through the spiracles of the prothorax.

They live principally on the bottom and feed on single-celled algae and detritus. They use the shovel-like tarsi of their forelegs to scrabble up their food from the bottom. They can also pierce strings of algae and suck out the contents. The hind legs act as oars for these excellent swimmers. They fly equally well. They shoot up from the depths with powerful strokes of their legs, break through the surface and fly away.

During mating in the spring, the males of many species chirp quite loudly. To do this they stroke the bristly covering of the top segment of the foreleg over the edge of the head. The eggs are laid singly on water-plants. The larvae hatch in the early summer and moult five times. In some species two generations may develop if conditions are favourable. With the exception of the three very minute *Micronecta* species, which live along the banks of ponds, lakes and streams, the lesser water-boatmen spend the winter as adults.

For further reference see:

Southwood, T. R. E., and Leston, D. (1959). *Land and Water-bugs of the British Isles*. Wayside and Woodland Series, Warne, London.

Macan, T. T. (1958). A Revised Key to the British Water-bugs (Hemiptera–Heteroptera). *Fresh-water Biological Association Scientific Publication No. 16*.

BEETLES (*Coleoptera*)

(i) *Dytiscidae*

Today it is generally held that the Dytiscids have developed from forms similar to the ground-beetles, Carabidae. In Britain there are about 106 species that inhabit still and flowing water of very varied types. Their external structure shows clearly how well they are adapted to aquatic life. The flattened, streamlined body has neither bristles nor projections which could hinder progress through the water. The posterior edge of the head fits exactly into the thorax, which in turn fits closely to the modified front wings (elytra). Not

Figure 20. Metacoxae of *Dytiscus marginalis*

even the large compound eyes project beyond the boat-shaped outline of the body. The body is completely covered with an oily, water-repellent secretion from numerous glands in the skin. The hind legs have wide, flattened segments with long, dense, swimming hairs and are excellent oars.

When taking air, the beetle rises to the surface with the tip of the abdomen uppermost, holding its hind legs forwards and upwards. It then breaks the surface with its claws. Air is taken into the tracheal system through the last two spiracles. In respiration, the air escapes through the outer spiracles into the space between the elytra and the abdomen, forming a bubble, which is used to regulate the buoyancy of the insect. In winter, when the beetles are cut off from the atmospheric air by a layer of ice, the air-store under the elytra is re-oxygenated by being pushed out at the end of the abdomen as a bubble. Oxygen dissolved in the water then diffuses into the bubble, thus restoring the equilibrium upset by the insect's respiration. By the same token, carbon dioxide escapes from high concentration in the bubble to low concentration in the water.

All Dytiscids are voracious carnivores, and they will attack any animal of their own size. The larger species attack tadpoles and even young fish. The males of many Dytiscids have the first three tarsal segments of the forelegs markedly widened and have specially formed hairs or stemmed suckers of varying length. With these they cling to the thorax of the female when mating. Many species lay their eggs individually or in strings on the surface of water-plants or preferably in the axils of leaves. Others bury them with the ovipositor in parts of plants just below the water surface. A third group lay their eggs on land in damp hiding-places, such as tree trunks or moss-covered stones close to the bank.

The larvae are easily recognised by the strange shape of their mouth-parts. Their large, curved mandibles are hollow. In them runs a single canal, which is formed from a groove on the inside that has become wholly enclosed. These channels connect directly with the throat. The remaining mouth-parts are stunted and the narrow mouth-opening is probably functionless. The larvae are carnivorous. Once the prey has been seized with the mandibles, a yellowish-brown fluid containing enzymes is poured out through the mandible channels, and in a few minutes the prey is paralysed and all its internal organs are dissolved. The food which has thus been digested outside the body is then sucked back into the larva through the channels.

The larvae also breathe air, which they take from the surface through two spiracles on the last abdominal segment. The habits of Dytiscid larvae vary according to their way of life. Crawling larvae usually live in small areas of water, ponds or streams. They can only swim very inadequately, and in order to breathe they support themselves on the bottom. The swimming species usually hold fast to water-plants when taking air. The floating forms can hang freely at the water surface. The burrowing larvae dig the front half of their bodies into the mud of very shallow water, leaving their abdomens sticking out above the water surface. The duration of development varies according to species. The mature larvae climb on to the bank and dig hollows in the soil, in which they pupate. Dytiscid beetles spend the winter as adults, as larvae or in the egg stage. The large species can live for up to five years. During mating or when seeking out habitats suitable for egg-laying or wintering in, they may undertake long flights overland.

(ii) *Haliplidae*

This family of small beetles is related to the Dytiscidae and has eighteen species in Britain. They are found chiefly in water with abundant vegetation. The beetles, which are at most 4 mm. long and seldom more than 2 mm. wide, can easily be recognised by two characteristics: when swimming they do not move all their legs simultaneously, but move each pair of legs on its own; on the ventral side the first joint of the third pair of legs is expanded into a large plate, which meets in the middle and laterally reaches to the edges of the elytron. It is notched on to the latter by a projection, which fits into a corresponding indentation (Figure 21). Between the ventral surface and the leg plates there is an air store.

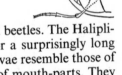

Figure 21. Ventral view of *Haliplus* sp., showing enlarged coxal plates

Respiration is similar to that of the Dytiscid beetles. The Haplidae can, however, remain under the water for a surprisingly long time. They feed chiefly on algae. Their slim larvae resemble those of the Dytiscid beetles and have the same form of mouth-parts. They bore with the mandibles into algae and suck out their contents. The mature larvae pupate in the bank in holes in the soil.

(iii) *Hydrophilidae*

Not all the genera of this large family are actually aquatic. Those that are live mainly in ponds and streams with abundant vegetation. The remaining genera live on the fringes between water and land or completely on dry land. Although the two families, Dytiscidae and Hydrophilidae, appear at first sight to resemble one another, there are important differences in their structure and way of life. For example, the backs of most Dytiscid beetles are flattened, while those of Hydrophilidae are domed. The middle and hind legs of the Hydrophilidae have only a sparse covering of hairs, and when swimming they are not moved simultaneously, but each pair of legs is moved separately. The Hydrophilidae swim very slowly, and the smaller species crawl. Like the Dytiscids, they breathe air from the atmosphere, but most of their air store is carried under the thorax and abdomen, where it is held by velvet-like hairs, and considerably less air is stored under the wings. For this reason, the smaller species are often seen swimming around upside-down, with their silvery, shiny abdomens uppermost.

They bring their heads to the surface to take air. On each side of the head there is a groove, consisting of two fringes of hair. The last four segments of the antennae are hollowed out and together form a hair groove, which, when laid against the head groove by bending the antennae, forms a complete tube, through which air is taken into the thoracic spiracles. Adult Hydrophilidae mainly eat plants. A few species lay their eggs singly in the water, but most species surround them with silken webs or cocoons. The females of a few species attach the egg cocoons to their hind legs and carry them around with them, while others attach them to water-plants. In some species the egg cocoon floats to the surface and is camouflaged by plant material woven into the cocoon wall. The cocoons of many species are provided with a hollow silken chimney or "mast", through which air may be taken when the egg is submerged.

The larvae live largely in shallow water. Most of them take air through two spiracles at the end of the body. All are predators. As they swim poorly and can only crawl slowly, they lie in wait for their prey, which is usually digested outside the body by means of regurgitated intestinal enzymes. The mandibles, however, do not have channels; there is therefore no waterproof connection between the throat and the food (as there is in the case of the Dytiscid beetles), and the prey is held out of the water to be eaten. Most species pupate in soil on the bank.

(iv) *Dryopoidea* (*Elminthidae* and *Parnidae*)

There are nineteen species of these very small brown or black beetles in Britain. They prefer fast-running water with plenty of oxygen. They feed principally on plants, particularly algae. They cannot swim, but creep along very slowly. Their method of breathing is of particular interest. After pupation on land, the beetle creeps back into the water and the store of air which it carries in its tracheal system and in the coating of hairs on the ventral surface must last for its entire life, for the adult never comes to the surface to take air.

The small supply of air must therefore constantly be regenerated. In order to do this, the beetle massages the hair-covering of the thorax with its forelegs from time to time by making brushing movements. This causes an air bubble to emerge from the spiracles of the prothorax and a smaller bubble from the metathorax and the first abdominal segment. The bubbles are then kneaded by the first segment and plates of the forelegs for about one and a half minutes to promote gas exchange between the bubbles and the water. The carbon dioxide in the used air is absorbed by the water and the bubble takes in oxygen from the water. Afterwards the bubble is sucked back into the spiracles. This somewhat complicated process explains why the Dryopoidea only live in fast-flowing or cold water with a high oxygen content.

The eggs are laid by the female (using the long ovipositor) in cracks in stones, under the crust of algae or in *Sphagnum* moss. The flat larvae have a fairly solid, chitinous covering and in many species are found in the same place as the adult beetles throughout the year. They breathe through tracheal gills, which are situated in a cavity (which can be closed) on the last abdominal segment.

(v) *Gyrinidae*

The whirligig beetles can be recognised immediately by their habit of swimming fantastically fast in circles or spirals on the surface of still or gently-flowing water. Their wide, flat middle and hind legs have long swimming hairs on the tarsi which fold up like fans. They are probably the most perfect swimming legs among water-insects. In fine weather the whirligig beetles like to sun themselves on floating leaves and stones on the bank. In the dusk they often undertake flights. They can, however, also dive like lightning deep into the water, where they have to cling to water-plants if they do not want to return like corks to the surface. They also use their forelegs to seize prey, which consists of living and dead animals on the surface of the water. As an adaptation to their life on the surface, their compound eyes are divided into two by a diagonal furrow, making an upper and a lower half, which differ in their anatomical structure. The upper part is used to see above the surface; the lower observes what passes below the surface.

The eggs are laid in May and June on roots, etc., under the water. The slim, carnivorous larvae hatch in June or July, and usually creep about on the bottom, but they can also swim quite skilfully by flapping the abdomen up and down. They breathe through tracheal gills, which are hair-like appendages on the abdomen. The adults usually spend the winter on land under stones or in leaf axils of plants along the bank. There are twelve species in Britain.

For further reference see:

Balfour-Browne, F. *British Water Beetles*. 3 vols. (1940, 1950, 1958). Ray Society, London.

Balfour-Browne, F. *Coleoptera. Hydradephaga. (Handbooks for the Identification of British Insects)*, Vol. IV, No. 3. Royal Entomological Society.

Bechyne, J. *Guide to Beetles.* Thames and Hudson, London, 1959.

Holland, D. G. (1972). A Key to the Larvae, Pupae and Adults of the British Species of Elminthidae, *Freshwater Biological Association Scientific Publication No. 26.*

TRUE FLIES (*Diptera*)

The number of flies whose larvae and pupae live in the water is so extraordinarily large that only the most important families can be briefly mentioned here.

1. MIDGES, MOSQUITOES AND CRANE-FLIES (*Nematocera*)

(i) MIDGES (*Chironomidae*)

The midges probably represent the freshwater insect family with the most species. About 400 species are known in Britain. There is practically no area of water, however small, salty, polluted or fast-flowing, which does not house at least one species of midge. They occur in huge numbers. The larvae often comprise 50–70% of the total deep fauna of lakes, and often in a density of more than 3,000 larvae per square metre. They provide one of the most important sources of food for fish. All species are very similar in their structure, so that identification is extremely difficult. Usually the larva, pupa and adult are needed to make an accurate identification.

The size varies between 1 and 2 mm. and about 20 mm., according to the species and age of the larva. They can be white, yellowish, green, blue-green or, when the blood fluid contains haemoglobin, light to dark red in colour. The two prolegs on the first thoracic segment as well as those at the end of the body make it possible for the larva to creep slowly, rather like a caterpillar. They breathe principally through the cuticle, but may use in addition two pairs of thin tubes on the penultimate abdominal segment, but not the four so-called "anal gills" at the end of the body, which are for the regulation of the concentration of body fluids. Most midge larvae live in the surface mud layer at the bottom of ponds or lakes. There they construct U-shaped tubes which are open at both ends at the surface of the mud. Many species—especially those that live in flowing water—construct elaborate houses, attached to water-plants. Others bore into the leaves of weeds. Many midge larvae feed on living and dead plankton algae, others on fresh plant tissue, many on rotten wood. The sub-family Tanypodinae are carnivores and do not spin tubes, but live freely. The pupae correspond to the general basic type of midge pupa. The adult life is solely devoted to reproduction. The males have densely-feathered antennae, while those of the females are filamentous. The eggs are grouped together in jelly-like masses. They are usually dropped by the flying female directly into the water.

For further reference see:

Bryce, D. Studies on the Larvae of British Chironomidae (Diptera), with Keys to the Chironomidae and Tanypodinae. *Trans. Soc. Brit. Ent.*, **14**, 19 (1960).

(ii) *Ceratopogonidae*

There are about 100 species in this family, but it is difficult to say how many of them are aquatic. The larvae of many genera live in moss, in wound exudations from trees, as well as in very varied types of water. They are up to 15 mm. in length, and usually live among algae or at the bottom of the water. They can swim quite well, and are mainly predaceous on other midges. The minute adults are rarely larger than 2 mm. They suck the blood of both insects and warm-blooded animals. Their bite is very painful for man. During midsummer the females lay their eggs, grouped in clumps, on algae and other water-plants or in 3–4-cm.-long strings on the surface of the water.

(iii) GNATS AND MOSQUITOES (*Culicidae*)

Of this family we are principally interested in the common mosquitoes of the genus *Culex* and the genus *Anopheles*. They are generally known for their nuisance value. Usually only the females bite. They have to suck blood to enable their eggs to mature, and they live as adults only for about six weeks. The males do not live as long, and feed chiefly on flower nectar and water. On summer evenings they swarm over the meadows, on river-banks, often over any raised objects, such as trees, haystacks, boat-houses and even the heads of people. These swarms consist mainly of males, while the females sit calmly on the leaves of the bushes along the banks or the reeds. As soon as a female flies into the swarm, several males leap on her, and one of them succeeds in mating with her. The mating lasts only a few seconds, during which time the partners generally drop to the grass.

The female *Anopheles* lays her elliptical eggs individually. Their walls have air-filled chambers, which keep the eggs floating on the surface. The female *Culex* lays her eggs in groups of 200 to 300 in egg-rafts. The larvae live in the surface layers of standing water. Their mouth-parts have long, soft hairs which beat constantly, creating two whorls of water, which draw food particles to the mouth. A remarkable selection of foodstuffs, such as algae, is made and unsuitable detritus particles drop out between the mouth-parts. *Anopheles* larvae can turn their heads through 180°, and thus feed off the underside of the water surface.

On the eighth abdominal segment of the *Culex* larvae is a breathing tube which branches upwards. At its tip it has the two openings of the tracheal system, each of which is surrounded by five triangular chitinous points; by closing over the aperture when the mosquito is submerged these prevent water from entering the breathing tube. The larvae always hang more or less vertically at the surface, with the relatively heavy head downwards. *Anopheles* larvae largely resemble the *Culex* larvae in body structure and way of life, but they do not have the breathing tube. The two openings of the tracheal system are in a shallow indentation on the dorsal side of the eighth abdominal segment. The larvae therefore lie horizontally under the surface of the water, to which they hang by means of several groups of hairs. The larvae moult four times. The pupae, which are very similar in both genera, also float on the surface, but they do not hold the head downwards: the powerful head and thorax are attached to the surface by two so-called "breathing horns". The pupae swim with jerky beats of the abdomen, although they can normally hang completely still on the surface.

The phantom midge *Chaoborus crystallinus* also belongs to this family, although the rostrum of the adult is too short and weak to suck blood. A special characteristic is the hair on the wings. The life of the adults is very short. As in *Culex* spp., the individual eggs are stuck together in rafts. The larvae live in ponds, especially on high moors. They are so transparent that all the body organs can be seen through the cuticle. They have no spiracles and breathe directly through the cuticle. They seize their prey (small Crustacea) with their antennae, which are specially formed as traps. They do not hang at the surface of the water, but float completely horizontally in various depths, aided by two pairs of air-sacs, which project from the two main tracheal trunks in the thorax and in the seventh abdominal segment. Their pupae can immediately be recognised in contrast to those of the other species by the fact that the abdomen is not curved under the head and thorax, but hangs relatively straight.

For further reference see:

Marshall, J. F. (1938). *The British Mosquitoes*. The British Museum, London.

(iv) BLACK-FLIES (*Simuliidae*)

The larvae of the black-flies live exclusively in flowing water, where they sit fast on stones or plants, attached by the sucker on the end of the abdomen. If they do become detached, they move forwards like caterpillars. The upper lip of the black-fly larvae has (on a shaft-like side piece on each side) one large and two small fans of fine, sometimes comb-like hairs. The fans together form a basket, with which the larvae filter their food—algae cells, detritus, etc.—out of the flowing water. The mature larvae spin conical pupal cases from the secretion of their salivary glands. From the opening, which always faces the current, two bundles of white threads project. These are the breathing organs of the pupae. Both sexes of the minute adults suck blood. In contrast with other mosquitoes, they are most active in bright sunshine. The wounds caused by their bites bleed longer than those of other mosquitoes. Mass attacks by black-flies in the Balkans and North America can lead to the death of cattle, brought on by heart failure after countless bites.

For further reference see:

Davies, L. (1968) and Smart, J. (1944). *Freshwater Biological Association Scientific Publications Nos. 24 and 9* respectively.

(v) *Dixidae*

The larvae of the main genus *Dixa* live in very shallow parts, on rocks over which the water flows, or on the floating leaves of water-plants. They can immediately be recognised by the U-bend of the body. When moving, the two arms of the U are pushed forward alternately. They have crawling welts on the ventral side. Air is absorbed through two spiracles on the back of the last abdominal segment. Special whirling organs on the head enable them to filter out particles of food from the water. The pupa is of the general midge type, but usually floats sideways on the water surface.

(vi) *Blepharoceridae*

This family is represented in Central Europe by the genus *Lipo-neura*, but there are no British species. Their larvae inhabit exclusively fast-flowing mountain streams, and they always sit on the rocks over which the water streams with most force. They attach themselves with the six large suckers on their ventral side and graze off the diatoms on the stones. The adult females catch insects, mainly midges, and suck them, while the males live on nectar.

(vii and viii) CRANE-FLIES OR DADDY-LONG-LEGS (*Tipulidae* and *Limnobiidae*)

These two families closely resemble each other (except for slight differences in the mouth-parts and the veining of the wings) which makes it impossible for the layman to distinguish them easily. The large and average species are readily recognised by their extraordinarily long legs and the V-shaped diagonal line on the back of the thorax.

The life of the adults is very short. They do not suck blood, but take nectar from flowers. One can see their small swarms most commonly at dusk on warm summer evenings over damp meadows and long the banks of water. Many species mate in flight, while others sit on firm surfaces. Usually, in doing so, both partners face in opposite directions. The females of some species bore their eggs into mud or damp soil with their ovipositors, others lay them on water-plants, while others drop them in flight into the water.

However much the adults resemble each other, this is not true of the larvae, which are found in very different habitats. A large number of the species live in damp soil or decomposing wood. Of the numerous aquatic animals, only a few of the most common can be mentioned here. Many *Tipula* larvae burrow in winding tunnels through the mud of shallow water, where they eat organic particles. Their abdomen ends in two open spiracles, which are surrounded by a rosette of chitinous projections. In shallow water the larvae commonly hang with this waterproof respiratory organ at the surface. Under water, the chitinous points bend together, enclosing an air bubble. Then the larvae breathe through the skin. For pupation, *Tipula* larvae usually dig vertical burrows in the bank.

The greatest number of mud-dwelling larvae among the *Limnobiidae* are similar to *Tipula*, except for the fact that their respiratory rosette is surrounded by at the most five and often only four appendages.

The *Dicranota* larvae live on the bottom of clear streams. They can creep quite skilfully with the aid of their five pairs of wartlike, clawed parapodia. They are predators and feed chiefly on worms (Tubificidae).

The larva of *Phalacrocera* is covered with long, forked, tracheal gills which make it look like the moss *Fontinalis*, on which it lives and feeds. The head can be completely retracted. They have no special organs for locomotion.

For further reference see:
Brindle, A. (1960). The Larvae and Pupae of the British Tipulidae, *Trans. Soc. Brit. Ent.*, **14**, 63.

(ix) *Ptychopteridae*

The larvae of the main genus, *Ptychoptera*, usually burrow in the mud or among dead leaves at the bottom of ponds or polluted streams. The two large body tracheae join at the posterior end to form a single, very thin, telescopic tracheal tube. It is almost as long as the body, and is always adjusted so as to bring the two spiracles to the surface of the water. When disturbed, it retracts the tail completely. If the water is temporarily too deep, the filamentous tracheal gills of the last segment are put into use, but they are inadequate for long periods of time. The larvae then crawl as soon as possible into shallower water, using the creeping welts at the edge of each segment.

(x) MOTH-FLIES (*Psychodidae*)

The adult moth-flies are only a few millimetres long and very densely haired, and look like very small moths. Their wings are laid together so as to form a ridged roof when at rest. The main genus is *Psychoda*. Their larvae live chiefly in much-polluted water, such as water-purification plants. They eat anything. Owing to the lack of oxygen in their habitat, they breathe atmospheric air through two spiracles in their breathing tube.

2. FLIES (*Brachycera*)

(i) HORSE-FLIES (*Tabanidae*)

The large horse-flies are generally well known. The males feed on nectar, but the females suck blood from warm-blooded animals. Some of the larvae live solely on the land; most of them prefer the damp regions along the banks of water; only a few are truly aquatic. These live chiefly on the bottom of shallow regions close to the bank, or among the plants on the surface of still water. The fourth to tenth segments of the larva bear pseudopods on thickened rings, which make the larva easily distinguishable. With the aid of these and the telescopic end of the abdomen, the animals can hold on to surfaces when crawling. They are predators and eat all types of water-animals, as well as snails and midge larvae.

(ii) *Stratiomyidae*

These flies can commonly be recognised by their black-and-yellow ringed abdomen. Only a few species are truly aquatic. Most common are those of the genus *Stratiomys*. They are found in springs or ponds, mostly in a dense mass of algae. The last abdominal segment is extended into a breathing tube and has two spiracles at the end, which are surrounded by a crown of long, feathery bristles. These are waterproof on top and open out when the larva is hanging at the surface of the water. When disturbed, they shut immediately, enclosing an air bubble, which the animal then takes down under the water with it. When it returns to the surface, this air bubble breaks the surface membrane and the fan reopens. The small, hooked upper jaws have a row of bristles and are used both for trapping food and for locomotion. The pupa floats horizontally at the surface of the water, but cannot be distinguished externally from the larva, because it is found inside the skin of the last larval stage.

(iii) HOVER-FLIES (*Syrphidae*)

The family of hover-flies embraces several thousand species. Only the sub-family of the Eristalinae interests us here, the adults of which look very like bees. Particularly in autumn, these plump flies can commonly be seen sitting on flowers or engaged in laying their longish-oval white eggs in decomposing material or along the banks of slow-flowing streams.

The larvae of the main genus *Tubifera* (*Eristalis*) live in stagnant or gently-flowing water with abundant foodstuffs, especially in drain ditches and settling tanks. Sometimes they are found in brackish water-pools or inland salt-water tanks. They have a thin, whitish, almost transparent skin, and can move quite actively by bending the body and using the seven pairs of hooked foot warts on the ventral surface. Sometimes the larvae burrow in the mud and sometimes they float on the surface, but they usually creep slowly along the bottom. A filter mechanism in the throat holds back firm mud particles, collects them into little balls and releases them from time to time backwards into the gut. During this, the mouth is closed and the water is passed into a special throat chamber, later to be pushed out again through the mouth.

Tubifera (*Eristalis*) larvae can live for a long time without direct access to air, the gas exchange occurring through the skin. Normally, they absorb air through the two spiracles at the end of their telescopic breathing tube, which reaches to the surface of the water. The extension of this breathing tube is effected by blood pressure, and it is retracted by means of powerful muscles. Thus the larvae can suit the length of their breathing tubes to the depth of the water, up to a maximum length of 10 cm. This remarkable organ has earned them the name of "rat-tailed maggot". They spend the winter as larvae, buried in the mud, and creep on to land to pupate in the spring. Inside the larval skin, which hardens to form the puparium, the pupa develops in about fourteen days, and from this the fly then hatches.

(iv) *Ephydridae*

By no means all Ephydrid larvae are aquatic, but the *Ephydra* species is remarkable for its resistance to the most unfavourable living conditions. They always inhabit shallow water of almost any condition. The same species can be found in freshwater pools, along the banks of lakes, in brackish pools, saline tanks and salt lakes of very high salt concentration and a temperature of up to 40° C. Even periods of drought can be spent by the larvae buried in the mud.

They move slowly, using their eight creeping welts, and feed chiefly on single-celled algae, which are filtered by a method similar to that used by *Tubifera* (*Eristalis*). They absorb air through the spiracles of their forked breathing tube. By bending their body sideways, they can swim clumsily. The larvae creep on to the land to pupate, and there climb up grass-blades, to which they hold fast by means of a furrow-like constriction between the last two pairs.of foot welts. The adults seldom fly. They feed on organic detritus, algae cells, etc. The eggs are laid individually on the water surface.

For further reference see:

Johannsen, O. A. (1934–7). *Aquatic Diptera*. Part I: Nematocera, exclusive of Chironomidae and Ceratopogonidae (1934). Part II: Orthorrhapha, Brachycera and Cyclorrhapha (1935). Part III: Chironomidae (1937). New York.

Colyer, C. N., and Hammond, C. O. (1951). *Flies of the British Isles*. Wayside and Woodland Series. Warne, London.

DRAGON-FLIES (*Odonata*)

There are forty-three endemic species of dragon-flies in Britain. They are divided into two sub-orders. The damsel-flies (*Zygoptera*), which are small or medium in size, have a long, thin body. Their two pairs of wings are almost equal in size, and when at rest they are folded together over the back or held pointing diagonally backwards. When seen from above, the distance between the eyes is considerably greater than the width of a single eye. The hawker dragon-flies (*Anisoptera*) include the medium and large forms. Their bodies are stout, and the front and rear pairs of wings differ in size, and when at rest they are always held wide open. In three endemic families the eyes touch each other, but in the case of the *Gomphidae* the space between the eyes is less than the diameter of one eye.

The larvae of dragon-flies occur in very varied types of water, even in peat bogs, high mountain pools and springs. The larvae of *Libellula depressa* even survive weeks of drought when the pools dry up by burying themselves in the mud. The majority of species, however, prefer ponds with considerable plant life.

All dragon-fly larvae are carnivorous. They lie in wait (amongst plants or half buried in the mud) for their prey or else creep stealthily after it. The youngest larvae feed at first on single-celled animals; later on small Crustacea, worms and aquatic insects of all types. The older dragon-fly larvae attack water-lice, freshwater shrimps, tadpoles and young fish. The prey is seized by means of a specially constructed lower lip. This consists of two parts: the *submentum*, which is hinged to the underside of the head and which extends and retracts and extends back between the coxae of the front pair of legs, and the *mentum*, which is connected to the submentum by means of a flexible joint, and when at rest lies closely pressed against the submentum. The mentum can be flat or spoon-shaped; it always terminates in two side flaps, ending in sharply-pointed hooks (labial palps). Since this organ covers the other mouth-parts or even the whole of the underside of the head when at rest, it is often known as the mask (Figure 22). It can be shot out as soon as the prey comes within range, the fangs seizing the prey, which, by retracting the mask, is brought back to the jaws and chewed.

The most important respiratory organ of the larva is the rectum. On the inner side there are six double rows of tracheal gills, minute whitish leaflets. The number of these varies according to species, and up to 24,000 have been counted. The water is changed by the rhythmic contraction and expansion of the rectal walls. With very forceful expulsion of water, the larva can use the jet so produced to propel itself rapidly forwards, the legs being held against the sides

94

of the body. Zygopteran larvae swim slowly by serpentine movement of the body, while their legs enable them to crawl slowly. The
three slender, leaf-like appendages (caudal lamellae) at the end of
the abdomen of the damsel-flies act as tracheal gills, but they also
serve an important function as a rudder or steering organ.

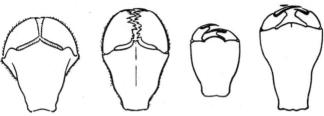

Figure 22. Masks (left to right): *Libellula* sp.; *Cordulegaster* sp.; *Gomphus* sp.;
Aeshna sp.

The number of larval stages varies between ten and fifteen,
according to the species and the ecological conditions of the habitat.
Similarly, the whole period of development of the larva (from
hatching to metamorphosis) can last from a few months up to five
years. There is no pupal stage in dragon-flies. When the larva is
fully grown, it stops feeding and crawls up the stem of a plant until
only the end of the abdomen is still submerged. Rectal respiration
is replaced by the intake of air through the spiracles of the thorax.

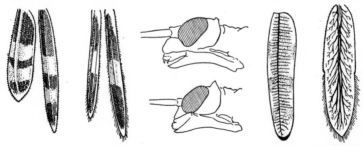

Figure 23. Left to right: Caudal gills of *Agrion splendens*; Caudal gills of *Agrion
virgo*; Head of the larva *Agrion splendens*; Head of the larva *Agrion virgo*; Caudal
gill of *Lestes* sp. and *Coenagrion* sp.

Finally, the larva crawls right out of the water, usually in the early
morning, and clings so tightly to the plant that later the empty
larval skin remains suspended there. A layer of air has gradually

been built up between the skin of the larva and the fully mature insect beneath. The pressure from this causes the larval skin of the thorax to burst along a longitudinal line. Out of this split emerges the thorax with the wings, followed by the head and the legs, and finally the abdomen. The position of the body during emergence differs in the various families. It lasts between three-quarters of an hour and about two hours. Subsequently, it takes one to two hours for the body and wings to harden sufficiently for the dragon-fly to attempt flight. The body colouring usually does not appear in its full glory for several days and normally only develops after feeding. The dragon-flies are among the most skilful creatures in flight. The larger species can attain a speed of up to 15 m. a second. They can hover in the air and even fly backwards for short distances. The ability to move both pairs of wings alternately gives them much of their skill in flying.

Dragon-flies are predators which hunt their prey on the wing. They seize butterflies, beetles, flies, midges, wasps and even smaller animals of their own kind in flight, and if they are not too heavy they eat them without alighting. The males of certain species of the larger dragon-flies have definite territories, from which they drive out other males of the same species who have ventured in, often with violent fighting. The females of many dragon-flies hunt their prey some distance from their home water, over meadows or in glades in woods.

The mating of dragon-flies, which can easily be observed, takes the following general pattern, but with minor variations, according to the individual species: as soon as a sexually mature male sees a female of his own species, he flies towards her. First, he seizes the female with his legs and then grasps the back of her head (in *Anisoptera*) or the thorax (in *Zygoptera*) with his anal claspers. The pair then flies off in tandem. Meanwhile, the male bends up the end of his abdomen to his second abdominal segment without releasing the female. In this position he fills his copulative organ with sperm and then straightens up again. Next the female bends her abdomen under and up and clings fast to the male genitalia. The pair then fly in tandem until mating is complete.

After mating the male releases the female or accompanies her to the egg-laying site. This varies according to the species. The eggs are laid above or below the surface of the water, among the plants, buried in the mud, and in the case of some species they are even ejected into the water during flight. In the case of a few *Zygoptera*,

96

the female sometimes goes below the water. The number of eggs laid can vary from a few hundred to more than 1,500, according to species.

For further reference see:

Corbet, P. S., Longfield, C., and Moore, N. W. (1960). *Dragon-flies*. The New Naturalist Series. Collins, London. (The appendix contains a key to the larvae.)

Frazer, F. C. (1949). *Handbooks for the Identification of British Insects: Odonata*. Royal Entomological Society of London.

ALDER-FLIES (*Megaloptera*)

In Britain the four-winged alder-flies are represented by only two species, *Sialis lutaria* L. and *S. fuliginosa* Pict. The adults often sit in large numbers in early summer on reeds and bushes along the banks. They do not fly readily, and then only in the dusk; they usually creep about slowly on vegetation. The females usually mate several times with different males. They lay their eggs on leaves and stems above the surface of the water, and preferably on reeds. The hatching larvae fall into the water or crawl in. The long, segmented, haired abdominal appendages of the larvae are tracheal gills.

The larvae live in the mud at the bottom, often at considerable depths in the most varied types of water, even in those with considerable organic pollution, provided that there is no risk of it drying up. They are skilful predators, their prey consisting of midge larvae, small mussels and worms. During their two-year period of development they moult nine times. In order to pupate, they crawl up on to the land and bury themselves in holes in the ground, often at a considerable distance from the bank.

LACE-WINGS (*Neuroptera*)

Only a very few of these flies live in the water as larvae, of which the "sponge-fly" *Sisyra* is shown here as an example. It lives on the surface of colonies of freshwater sponges and Polyzoa. When crawling, it uses its long, thin antennae as stilts. The upper and lower jaws are elongated into fine half-tubes, which, when placed together, form two closed sucking tubes. With these the larva bores into the body of the sponges or Polyzoa and sucks out their liquid contents. On the ventral surface of the abdomen there are seven pairs of almost identical tracheal gills.

In early summer the larvae creep up the stems of plants and pupate just above the water surface in grey, egg-shaped cocoons.

The small black or brown adults move only at dusk. The females attach their eggs to parts of plants above the water and coat them in a white silken web. From there the young larvae fall into the water and swim to the host colony.

For further reference see:

Kimmins, D. E. (1962). Keys to the British Species of Aquatic Megaloptera and Neuroptera, *Freshwater Biological Association Scientific Publication No. 8* (2nd edition).

AQUATIC MOTHS (*Lepidoptera*)

To the non-specialist it may appear surprising that the Lepidoptera are even mentioned in a book on freshwater animals. In the adult stage, only the wingless females of *Acentropus niveus* live wholly in the water, and only for mating with the winged males do they stretch the abdomen above the water surface. Curiously, this species also has winged females which fly about normally in the air. On the other hand, there are several moth species whose development from egg to pupa takes place in the water, while the adults live in the air. As an example of the true aquatic moth, *Nymphula* (*Hydrocampa*) *nymphaeata* has been illustrated here. After mating, the female settles on a floating leaf to lay her eggs, bends her abdomen over the edge and attaches the eggs in rows to the underside of the leaf. The young larvae feed on the tissue of the floating leaves, principally those of *Potamogeton* sp. They soon seize a small leaf, possibly that of duckweed, and cover themselves with it while they remain sitting on the underside of the floating leaf.

Later, towards the end of the summer, the larvae, which have grown in the meantime, cut from the floating leaves two larger, almost elliptical pieces and spin them to each other with the long edges together. They spend the autumn in these water-filled houses. The houses are not waterproof, and so the caterpillar's spiracles are closed. Respiration takes place through the skin. The larvae spend the winter at the bottom, and in the following spring they climb to the surface again and, as they grow, build themselves ever larger sheaths. Finally, after a moult, the spiracles open, the finely-haired skin becomes water-repellent and the sheath is filled with air from then onwards. In summer the sheath is about 4 cm. long and 2–3 cm. wide. The caterpillar pupates in August. The pupal housing is similar to that of the caterpillar, and is woven on to plant stems below the water surface. The plant stem is woven so closely between the two side walls of the cocoon that the latter stand out like wings from the stem. Air collects in the cocoon and, on hatching, the moth takes the bubble under its wings and is shot to the surface like a cork. It runs across the surface to the bank and takes its first flight shortly afterwards.

PARASITIC WASPS (*Hymenoptera*)

Some parasitic Hymenoptera must also be added to this account of the aquatic insects. Some Ichneumonidae, Braconidae and Agriotypidae lay their eggs in many types of water-insects or their larvae. The adults creep about under the surface of the water in order to lay their eggs. However, they rarely show in their body structure any characteristics which could be regarded as adapting them to this partially aquatic life.

The example illustrated is *Agriotypus armatus*. In the spring the tiny females of this species seek out caddis larvae, mostly those of *Silo* and *Goëra*, and lay one egg in each larva. The young *Agriotypus* larva feeds on the host larva, but does not damage its main organs. Only after the caddis larva has pupated do they consume the host entirely. Then the *Agriotypus* larva spins a strip of silk 1–2 mm. wide and 10–50 mm. long. Before pupating, it pushes this strip out of the cocoon, which makes the parasitised caddis-fly cocoon readily recognisable. The function of this strip is still a matter of speculation, although it may be respiratory, since the *Agriotypus* pupae die if the strip is removed.

CADDIS-FLIES (*Trichoptera*)

The caddis-flies belong to the Trichoptera, which literally means "hairy-winged", and as adults they look rather like small moths. Their larvae are, with one exception, aquatic; owing to their habit of living in cases of their own construction, they are familiar fresh-water animals. There are about 650 described species of caddis-fly in Europe today, and 190 in Britain.

Caddis larvae can be divided into two main groups. In those with eruciform larvae the longitudinal axis of the head forms a right angle with the body axis, while in those with campodeid larvae the head and body axis are in a straight line. There are also other differences in the body structure and habits of the two groups.

All eruciform caddis larvae have a case. They always carry it around with them and never voluntarily leave it as it protects their soft abdomen. When in danger, they can withdraw completely into the case. Basically, the case consists of a tube of silken web. The powerful spinning glands of the larvae secrete a fluid which hardens into elastic threads in the water. These are then woven into the case with the forelegs and mouth-parts. The casing of the very young larva consists mainly of silk woven with the jelly of the egg. Only later does the larva begin to coat the silk case on the outside with foreign material, typical of the species, always building on to the front end.

As the larva grows, so the casing must be increased in size. The older, and therefore narrower, part at the back is then no longer inhabited, and is generally bitten off by the animal. The cases are built from all sorts of material: pieces of reed, fresh or decayed leaves and grass blades, pine needles, small empty snail or mussel shells, seeds, pieces of twig, sand grains or small stones. Generally, those larvae that live in still or slow-flowing water build their cases of light plant material, while those that live in streams with a faster current select heavier building materials, such as stones and sand. The various species do in fact prefer quite specific materials, but they may change them according to their habitat, the season or the age of the larva. The composition of the case can therefore only be used as an indication of the family to which the larva belongs, and perhaps its genus, but never the species. Much more constant, however, is the manner in which the materials are used; for example, larvae of species which arrange their materials diagonally *never* place them longitudinally.

All eruciform caddis larvae are vegetarians, feeding on algae, detritus and fresh or decomposed particles of higher plants. They use string-like tracheal gills for breathing. These are situated on the back, at the side or in rows underneath the abdomen, according to the species. They may be arranged individually, in pairs or in threes, or even grouped bunches. Species without gills are rare.

Only a few species with campodeid larvae have cases. They live almost exclusively in running water, streams, rivers or larger lakes. Many are predators, which prowl around freely and feed on all sorts of small water-animals, but the majority spin net-like webs of various shapes between stones or water-plants (Figure 24). These nets are used for trapping, and are usually connected with a silk-spun tunnel in which the larva sits waiting for suitable prey to be caught. The nets are usually hung with detritus, and so are often difficult to find.

The adult larvae pupate in suitable hiding-places—under stones, roots, etc. The larvae which carry cases close the front and rear openings of their case, leaving only small holes for respiration, and

100

then attach it firmly to the ground. The larvae without cases also build cocoons. The pupal stage lasts for about two or three weeks before it leaves its housing, with antennae, legs and wing outgrowths now well developed. It now swims or climbs up water-plants to the surface. Once at the surface, the pupal skin breaks and the winged adult insect emerges.

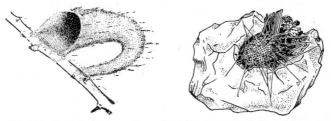

Figure 24. Net of caddis-fly larva *Neureclipsis bimaculata* L. (left) and *Hydropsyche* sp. (right)

The caddis-flies are often confused with small moths, to which they bear a superficial resemblance. The smaller species are about the same size as clothes moths, while the largest *Phryganea* sp. are about the size of the Brimstone butterfly. However, when resting, the caddis-fly always lays its wings in a roof-like position along the abdomen. The two insect orders Trichoptera and Lepidoptera are undoubtedly closely related historically, although the caddis-flies have neither proboscis nor flattened scales on their wings. They are

Figure 25. Head of the larva *Anabolia* sp. (left) and dorsal view of the head and thorax of the larva *Lepidostoma hirtum* (right)

generally dull in colour—grey, black, brown—but some species also have a red or yellow patterning. The thin, many-segmented antennae are often longer than the body itself, and when the insect is at rest they are held stretched out forwards.

During the day the adults generally stay in hiding-places not far from the water; only at dusk do they emerge and fly clumsily around. Individual adults do not generally live for more than about a week. They are on the wing for from three to four weeks from the beginning of June to the end of August.

The eggs can be round or oval and are green or yellow in colour. They are grouped in batches of a few dozen or several hundred, according to species. In many species the female lays the eggs by flying just above the surface of the water and simply letting the packets of eggs drop. Others attach them to grass or leaves which overhang the surface of the water, so that when they hatch the young larvae fall into the water. Females of some species, especially those with campodeid larvae, crawl into the water and attach their eggs to stones or water-plants below the surface. Often the jelly covering the eggs swells up in the water to the size of a cherry.

Finally, there is one British caddis-fly larva, *Enoicyla pusilla* Burm., which does not live in water, but in damp moss on banks, under hedges or on tree trunks. It does not breathe through tracheal gills, but possesses an open tracheal system.

For further reference see:

Hickin, N. E. (1952). *Caddis*. Field Study Books. Methuen, London.
Hickin, N. E. (1967). *Caddis Larvae*. Hutchinson. London.
Mosely, M. E. (1949). *The British Caddis-flies* (*Trichoptera*). Routledge, London. (This book is entirely concerned with the adult stage.)

Freshwater Snails, Limpets and Mussels (*Mollusca*)

MUSSELS (*Lamellibranchiata*)

In British waters there are twenty-six species of mussel, which are grouped in the families Unionidae, Sphaeriidae and Dreissenidae. In the mud of shallow, calm shores one can often see long furrows, at the end of which sits a mussel. These tracks give evidence of the movement of the mussels, which, on account of their slowness, can otherwise only be observed with considerable patience. They move by means of the muscular foot, which in the Unionidae resembles a plough-share, but in the other two families is more tongue-shaped. In locomotion the foot first becomes distended as a result of blood pressure and then stretches out forwards between the two valves of the shell. Next its muscles contract and the whole mussel is pulled forward. The Unionidae use the foot to bore into the mud, but in the other two families it adheres with the aid of abundant slime to the surface over which it travels. It is difficult to observe any sign of life in these animals, whose bodies are entirely surrounded by a double-valved shell.

In the aquarium we can immediately see that even when the shell is closed there are two openings at the rear end. Through the lower one a current of water enters, taking with it suspended particles of food—the smallest plankton plants and animals as well as detritus. After respiration, the water and faeces are discharged through the upper opening. In the Unionidae both openings are slit-like. In *Dreissena* and *Sphaerium* their edges are drawn out into tubes (siphons). In the *Pisidae* the lower opening is in the form of a slit and the upper in the form of a siphon. The soft parts of the mussel are surrounded by a thin cloak of skin, called the "mantle", the edge of which secretes the shell. Under the mantle on each side of the body are the gills. They consist of two leaves, each composed of two lamellae, which are made up of numerous ciliated and partly-converging threads. The gills are not only used for breathing. Their slime-covered, ciliated epithelium snatches food particles out of the water (as do the outer sides of the mantle and the foot), and then leads the particles along a specific route to the mouth, which is situated above the foot at the anterior end.

The Unionidae and the Dreissenidae have separate sexes. As far as we know, *Anodonta* forms hermaphrodites in small, enclosed lakes. The Sphaeriidae are always hermaphrodite. The Dreissenidae discharge their sperm and eggs into the water, where fertilisation takes place. From the fertilised eggs small plankton-like larvae develop, with a bunch of cilia at the anterior end. The Sphaeriidae are viviparous. The sperm cells are taken into the body with the respiratory current. The fertilised eggs fix themselves in the inner gill lamella, the tissues of which form brood pouches. The young— seldom more than a dozen from each mother—are not discharged for about a year. They are then well developed and sometimes even sexually mature.

In the Unionidae the sperm cells are released into the water and carried in with the respiratory water current to the gills, to which the eggs have come from the ovaries. The fertilised eggs develop into larvae in special brood pouches, modified from gill tissue. These larvae, called *Glochidia*, are only about 0·25 mm. long and have two valves which are connected by a closing muscle (Figure 26). They are expelled into the water by the mother. To develop further, the *Glochidia* or larvae of *Anodonta* must attach themselves to the fins of fish by means of the hooks on the edge of their shells, whereas the *Glochidia* of *Unio* and *Margaritifer* are swallowed whole by fish and stick fast in their gills. The host's tissue now encloses and feeds

103

the small parasites for several weeks. Naturally, such a complicated form of development requires a vast number of eggs: 200,000 to 400,000 are produced by *Unio* and *Anodonta* and about 1,000,000 by *Margaritifer*.

Figure 26. *Glochidium* larva of *Unio* sp.

Freshwater mussels play an important part in conserving the energy resources of the water in which they live, a fact which is often overlooked in studying them. They filter floating substances out of the water almost continuously and, after converting them into their body-tissues, they release them again into the mud on the bottom when they die. They are often found in relatively large numbers: up to ten per square metre is by no means rare. The quantity which each animal filters has been estimated for an American species as 42 litres of water per hour.

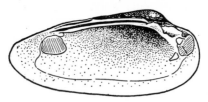

Figure 27. The left valve of the shell of *Unio* sp. The largest projection on the upper edge is the umbo. Beneath it, the pronounced projection is the cardinal hinge tooth; the lateral hinge teeth are the ridge formations on either side of it. The line running parallel with the edge of the shell (clearly visible in the living mussel shell) marks the edge of the mantle. The two rounded, shaded hollows on the inner side of each end of the shell are where the shell-closing muscles are attached

When observing the living animal creeping along the ground, it is simple to see which parts are the top, bottom, front and back, as well as right and left valves. The upper edges of the two valves are held together by a horny band which is elastic when the animal is alive. Attached to this band is the oldest and most markedly domed

104

part of the shell, called the "umbo". The inner sides of the upper edges of the valves are mostly lined with tooth-like projections and ridges, which fit into one another. The short, strong teeth near the umbo are the cardinal teeth; the teeth which run to the back or to both sides are the lateral teeth (Figure 27).

FRESHWATER SNAILS (*Gastropoda*)

1. PULMONATE SNAILS (*Basommatophora*)

All indigenous species have a lid-less shell and one pair of tentacles which cannot be retracted. The eyes are situated at the base of the tentacles.

(i) POND-SNAILS (*Limnaeidae*)

The pond-snails inhabit very varied types of water, but are mainly confined to those with a high calcium content. The form and, in part, the colouring of the shell differ according to the environment, sometimes quite markedly. The strength of the current, the average temperature, the chemical and food conditions of the water and, finally, the degree of infection by Trematode parasites produce very different local forms. This led in the past, before anatomical examinations of the soft body of the snail were undertaken, to the description of numerous species, most of which are now known to be only local varieties.

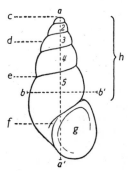

Figure 28. Diagram of a snail shell:
a–a′ Axis (height of shell)
b–b′ Width of shell
c Apex
d Single whorl
e Seam
f Umbilicus
g Aperture
h Whorls

The pond-snails creep along slowly on their foot, not directly on the ground, but on slime, which is continually secreted by glands at the front of the foot. Movement is achieved by the alternate regular contraction and relaxation of the various foot muscles. The large *Limnaea stagnalis* in particular can often be seen on the underside

105

of the water surface, the foot uppermost and the shell hanging downwards. Even so, the animal is moving along a band of slime attached to the water surface. Occasionally very small snails can be seen hanging from the surface by long threads of slime.

Pond-snails belong to the type of snails that feed by "grazing". Using the radula (a tongue-like organ inside the mouth, which looks and acts rather like a grater with even, thick rows of teeth) they scrape the algae covering from water-plants and stones. They also use their jaws to bite pieces of soft or decaying parts of plants and chew them with the radula. Occasionally they eat the carcasses or spawn of various water-animals and Polyzoa. Those living in deep water feed principally on detritus.

Pond-snails which inhabit still, shallow water breathe atmospheric air. To take air, they come to the surface, especially if the water is lacking in dissolved oxygen, and open the breathing aperture, which is kept closed when under water. They thus allow fresh air to enter their mantle cavity, the top of which is covered by a finely-branched lung. In winter, when ice covers the surface—and in the case of snails living in more rapidly-flowing, or deeper, water—this method of respiration is replaced by general diffusion of dissolved gases through the skin. If a *Limnaea* is disturbed when at the surface, it can expel the air from its breathing aperture and sink like a stone to the bottom. On the other hand, snails which crawl along the bottom can reduce the pressure of the air inside them by relaxing their mantle muscles, and if they then release their feet from the bottom they float up to the surface like corks.

Like all pulmonates, the pond-snails are hermaphrodite. In spite of this, self-fertilisation is rare under natural conditions, for, when mating, one animal acts as male and the other as female. The spawn consists of sausage-like jelly capsules, the upper sides of which are slightly domed, while the flat undersides adhere to stones or water-plants. The eggs are suspended on slim threads on the inner wall of the capsule. They hatch into small but fully formed snails.

(ii) RAMSHORN SNAILS (*Planorbidae*)

The ramshorn snails inhabit largely stagnant waters. The most well-known species is *Planorbis corneus*, which occurs commonly in ponds with plenty of plants, together with *Limnaea stagnalis*. They do not, however, live in the surface layers of the water, but rather on the bottom, so that detritus forms a larger part of their diet than in the case of the large pond-snails. The species that inhabit ponds graze off the algae and detritus at the surface. Characteristic of the ramshorn snails is the red colouring of their blood, due to the presence of haemoglobin. It is most marked in *P. corneus*, but in several smaller species it is hardly visible.

The breathing aperture in these snails is very extensive and is divided into front and back sections by a fold in the mantle. *P. corneus* surfaces for air much less often than *Limnaea stagnalis*, and in well-aerated water does not need to surface at all. On the left side of *P. corneus* there is a small projecting fold of skin, which presumably operates as a gill. This snail hibernates buried in the mud. The smaller ramshorns which live in ponds breathe atmospheric air so long as the water surface is not frozen over. When this occurs in winter, they change from breathing air to breathing water. They fill the breathing aperture with water, and the lung network then acts as a sort of gill.

The breathing apertures of *Planorbis* that live at the bottom of lakes are always full of water. If these animals, however, do get an opportunity of taking air at the surface, then they express the water from the lung by contracting the mantle muscles. Respiration through the skin does not appear to be common.

The ramshorn snails are hermaphrodite. Mating is always reciprocal, i.e. both partners act as both male and female simultaneously. The spawn is flat and cake-like. The number of eggs in each varies from five to about thirty, according to species, but is never large.

(iii) FRESHWATER LIMPETS (*Ancylidae*)

There are only two species in Britain (*Ancylastrum fluviatile* and *Ancylus lacustris*) which belong to this small group of pulmonates. The river limpet (*A. fluviatile*) is ideally adapted to life in fast-flowing water by its cap-like shell. It sits with the wide foot attached to stones and never comes to the surface. The lung aperture has completely disappeared and, although they are pulmonate snails, they respire wholly by diffusion through the skin. The spawn, shaped like an hour-glass and about 2–4 mm. in diameter, is firmly attached to stones. Each spawn mass contains about 100 eggs.

A. lacustris, the lake limpet, lives principally among the reeds on the edge of stagnant water. These limpets creep slowly up the reed stems, grazing on the coating of diatoms and blue-green algae. The lung aperture is missing here also and this limpet does not come to the surface to breathe, but relies entirely on skin respiration. The soft body is much smaller than the shell, which overhangs it like a roof. Only the tips of the tentacles project slightly beyond the edge of the shell. The eggs are laid in flat, transparent capsules of about 2–4 mm. in diameter. The capsules contain only very few eggs, at most about ten.

2. OPERCULATE SNAILS (*Prosobranchia*)

These snails can immediately be recognised by the horny plate which they carry on the foot. When they withdraw into their shell, this plate closes the shell aperture.

(i) NERITES (*Neritidae*)

This family contains many marine, brackish and freshwater species. The only indigenous species, *Theodoxus fluviatilis*, is fairly common in calcareous rivers and streams, particularly in the more rapid parts. The eyes are situated on the short stalks on the outside of the bristle-like tentacles. The sexes are separate. The egg capsules, which are white, the size of a pinhead and slightly domed, are laid on stones or mussel shells. They contain from seventy to ninety eggs, but only one of these develops into a larva, eating up the remaining eggs before leaving the egg capsule as a fully-developed snail.

(ii) FRESHWATER WINKLES (*Viviparidae*)

The main species, *Viviparus* (*Paludina*) *viviparus*, is the largest indigenous freshwater snail. It lives principally in still water, and may also occur in relatively acid water. Living on the bottom, it is primarily a detritus-feeder. The sexes are separate and can easily be distinguished. The right tentacle of the smaller male is shorter than the left and is thickly knobbed, as it contains the genital organ. Both tentacles of the female, on the other hand, are equally thin. As their name implies, they do not lay eggs, but produce their young fully developed. The eggs develop in the uterus, where the embryos feed on a milky fluid containing protein. The young are not born until they are fully developed and about 10 mm. long. Their shells have four whorls and are covered with bristles, which later fall off.

(iii) VALVE SNAILS (*Valvatidae*)

The small *Valvata* species, which are only up to 7 mm. in height, live in muddy streams and on the bottom of lakes. They are, however, occasionally found in various smaller areas of water. The head is extended into a snout; the front end of the foot is wide and divided into two flaps. The eyes lie behind the long, thin tentacles. When crawling about, the two-sided and feathery gill normally projects on the left side of the gill opening. These snails feed principally on detritus and occasionally on carcasses. So far as we know, they are hermaphrodite. However, very little is known about their reproduction.

(iv) *Hydrobiidae*

There are four genera in Britain belonging to this family, but their way of life is so different and in part completely unknown that a general treatment of this family is unsuitable here. The most important ones are illustrated.

In order to identify the shell of the snail, it is important to determine whether it winds to the right or to the left. In order to do this, the shell is held so that its aperture is towards the observer and the point directed upwards. If the opening is then to the right of a vertical line from the tip to the lower edge of the aperture, then the shell is said to wind to the right (dextral); if it is to the left, then the shell winds to the left (sinistral). Most shells are dextral, but the Physidae provide an example of shells that are sinistral. The terminology for the individual parts of the shell can be seen in Figure 28.

For further reference see:

Ellis, A. E. (1926). *British Snails*. Oxford.

Ellis, A. E. (1940). Freshwater Bivalves (Mollusca). Linnean Society of London. *Synopsis of the British Fauna*, No. 4.

Macan, T. T. (1960). A Key to British Fresh- and Brackish-water Gastropods. *Freshwater Biological Association Scientific Publication No. 13* (2nd edition).

Animal Life Illustrated

Sponges (*Porifera*)

51. Freshwater sponge. *Euspongilla lacustris* L. The most common native freshwater sponge. Colonies up to 20 cm. long. Identification of species only possible by examination of the gemmules and spicules under a microscope. Fairly common.

Hydroids (*Coelenterata*)

52. Freshwater hydra. *Hydra* sp. Common in still water on plants in ponds and lakes. About 10 mm. long, excluding tentacles. 2 species: *Hydra viridis* is green and *H. fusca* is brown.

53. Freshwater jellyfish. *Craspedacusta sowerbii* Lank. Free-swimming jellyfish; very rarely found in standing water and chiefly in the warm-water basins of hothouses. Diameter of umbrella from 0·6 to about 20 mm. From 8 to about 400 long tentacles, according to age and conditions of environment. The jellyfish form of the species is produced from buds on the polyp only 0·5–2 mm. long and lacking tentacles; formerly known as *Microhydra ryderi* Lank. It occurs individually or in small colonies.

54. *Cordylophora lacustris* Pall. Found in brackish water; Norfolk Broads and estuaries, including the London Docks; seldom in pure fresh water. Branched colonies with tentacles and reproductive buds. Up to 10 cm. high.

Moss Animalcules (*Polyzoa*)

55. *Cristatella mucedo* Cuv. Colonies in clear, standing water. Transparent and jelly-like. Mostly 2 to 3 cm., seldom larger, up to 5 cm. Statoblasts lens-shaped, with hooked spines. Fairly common.

56. *Plumatella fruticosa* Allm. Colonies. Found on floating leaves and water-plants in still and gently-flowing water. Characteristic is the regular branching of the chitin tubes. Up to about 10 cm. Statoblasts oval, usually with a ring of cilia. Fairly common.

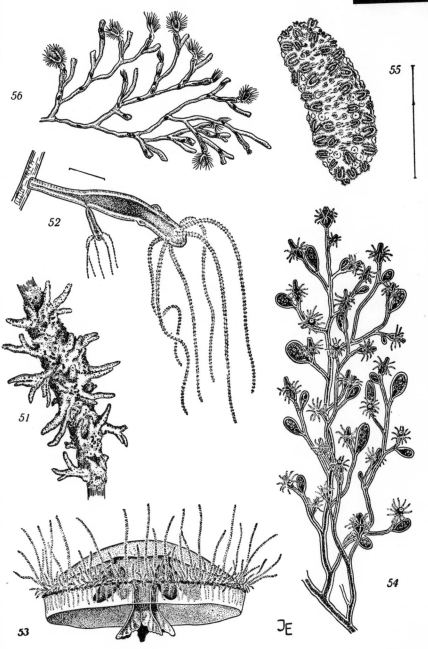

56

55

52

51

54

53

JE

Flatworms (*Platyhelminthes*)

(a) Rhabdocoela

57. *Mesostoma ehrenbergi* (Focke). (Family Typhloplanidae.) Locally abundant in stagnant water among plants. Leaf-like in shape; transparent. Up to 15 mm. in length. Pale brown with some of the organs yellow.

(b) Tricladida

58. *Dendrocoelum lacteum* (Müller). (Family Dendrocoelidae.) Common in streams and standing water. Milky white; gut often visible, and reddish-brown or greyish-black. Head end squared off with movable lateral lobes. 2 black eyes near anterior end; the distance between them is greater than that from each eye to the edge of the head. Up to 26 mm. long and 6 mm. wide.

59. *Polycelis nigra* (Ehrbg.). (Family Planariidae.) Very common in streams and standing water. Variable in colour, grey, black, brown, green red-brown, yellow. Head squared off, with slight bulge forwards in the centre. Numerous small eye-spots round the edges of the front end. Up to 12 mm. long and 1·5 mm. wide.

60. *Polycelis felina* (Dalyell). (Family Planariidae.) Found in springs and small streams of a constant low temperature. Colour as No. 59. Head with 2 awl-like tentacles. Numerous eye-spots round the edge. Up to 18 mm. long and 2 mm. wide.

61. *Crenobia alpina* (Dana). (Family Planariidae.) Often found in mountain streams, springs and small lakes. Prefers cold and avoids stagnant water. Mostly slate grey or black, less often brown, reddish, greenish, white or speckled. Head squared off, with 2 movable, outstretched tentacles. Two eyes set at same distance from the anterior end. Up to 16 mm. long and 5 mm. wide.

62. *Planaria torva* (O. F. Müller). (Family Planariidae.) In standing water and slow-running streams. Brown to black. Anterior end rounded off and blunt corners of head end rounding into the side edges. Lateral lobes of head not displaced. 2 eyes in large unpigmented areas. Up to 20 mm. long. Rare, N. Ireland and S.W. Scotland.

63. *Dugesia lugubris* (O. Schm.). (Family Planariidae.) Very common in standing water and slow-flowing streams. Fairly insensitive to changes in temperature and organic impurities. Mostly black, sometimes grey-brown. Head end rounded off and fairly broad, changes shape. 2 eyes set in front of the widest point of the head. Up to 20 mm. long and 4 mm. wide.

64. *Dugesia gonocephala* (Dug.). (Family Planariidae.) Found in clean, flowing water. Brown, grey, blackish, sometimes with dark longitudinal stripes. Head triangular, with small movable "ears" on each side. 2 eyes set in front of the broadest part of the head. The distance between the eyes is about equal to the distance from each eye to the edge of the head. Up to 25 mm. in length and 6 mm. in width. Common in north-west Europe, but not recorded in Britain.

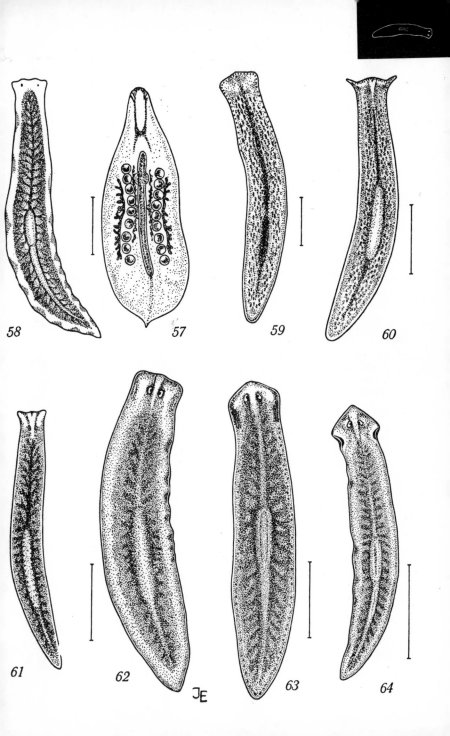

58   57   59   60

61   62   JE   63   64

Hairworms (*Nematomorpha*)

65. *Gordius aquaticus* Duj. (Family, Gordiidae.) Similar to tough horse-hair. Yellow, brown or black. Length up to 80 cm. Found on vegetation in stagnant water.

True Worms (*Annelida*)

FRESHWATER WORMS WITH BRISTLES (*Oligochaeta*)

66. *Chaetogaster diaphanus* (Gruithuisen). (Family Naidae.) Found on water-plants and in mud of standing and running water, also in brackish water. Transparent. Bristles only on the ventral side. 14 to 15 segments. Found in chains of animals up to 15 mm. long. Carnivorous. There are 4 other similar species in the genus.

67. *Stylaria lacustris* (L.). (Family Naidae.) Found on water-plants and in mud, chiefly in standing water, and also in water with a low salt content. Very transparent. Colour variable, in accordance with habitat and seasons. Front of body yellow to brown; rest of body with black rings. Always has eye-spots. Found in chains of animals up to 18 mm. long. Swims very well.

68. *Nais variabilis* (Piguet). (Family Naidae.) Found among water-plants and in mud of standing water, and also in brackish water. Light grey in colour. Eye-spots. Found in chains of up to 8 mm. long. Lives on algae. Swims well. 3 other similar species in the genus.

69. *Lumbricillus* sp. (Family Enchytraeidae, the pot worms.) Found close to the banks of both salt and severely polluted water. Yellowish to reddish-brown in colour. 3–8 bristles per bundle. 10–20 mm. in length. Many species.

70. Blood worms. *Tubifex* sp. (Family Tubificidae.) Found among the mud and sand at the bottom of standing, flowing and polluted water. They live in vertical tubes cemented with slime; the front end of the animal is fixed, while the tail projects and waves about. Red to reddish-yellow. The most common species is *Tubifex tubifex*, up to 85 mm. long. Has hair bristles. There are 7 genera and many species.

71. *Limnodrilus hoffmeisteri* Clap. (Family Tubificidae.) Same habits as *Tubifex*. Often found associated with latter. No hair bristles. Red to brownish-red in colour. Up to 50 mm. in length.

72. *Lumbriculus variegatus* (Müller). (Family Lumbriculidae.) Common among water-plants or at the bottom of standing water, especially in ponds in woods. Gut red to brown, visible through the greenish body. 40 to 100 mm. in length and 1–1·5 mm. thick. Similar to the earthworm. It constructs small mud tubes and often has its anterior end buried in the mud.

73. *Eiseniella tetraedra* (Savigny). (Family Lumbricidae.) The only aquatic species of the earthworm family. Found close to the banks of streams. Sienna brown in colour; more rarely yellow to red-brown. 30–50 mm. long and 2–4 mm. thick. Centre of body and tail square.

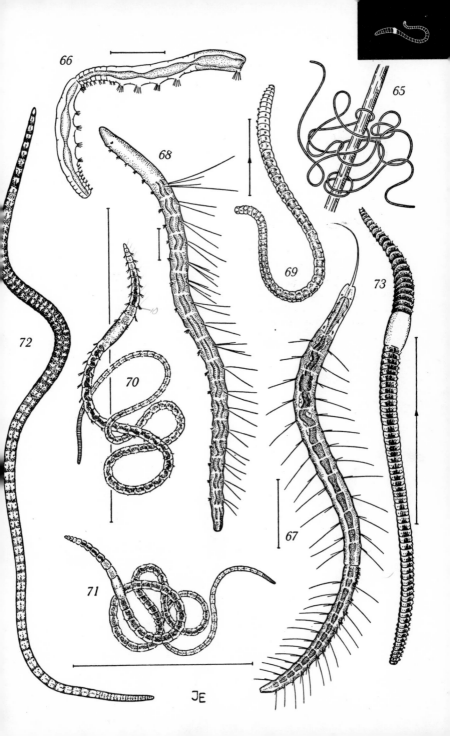

65

66

68

69

70

72

71

67

73

JE

Position of eyes (left to right): *Piscicola geometra; Hemiclepsis marginata; Haementeria costata; Glossiphonia complanata; Glossiphonia heteroclita; Helobdella stagnalis; Hirudo medicinalis; Erpobdella octoculata*

PLATE 4

This handsome Asian species of freshwater crayfish, *Astacus leptodactylus* Eschscholz, does not occur in Britain, although it does just spread into western Europe

PLATE 4

LEECHES (*Hirudinea*)

74. *Piscicola geometra* (L.). (Family Ichthyobdellidae.) Feeds on fish of very varied types, e.g. pike and perch. Both anterior and posterior suckers distinct from the body. Greenish-brown mottling. Up to 10 cm. long. Body at rest cylindrical and 10 times as long as it is broad. Swims well. Found in running water and on shores of large lakes.

75. *Hemiclepsis marginata* (O. F. Müller). (Family Glossiphoniidae.) Found in standing and running water. Sucks blood from fish and Amphibia. Back greenish- to reddish-brown, with transverse and longitudinal stripes of yellow spots. 4 longitudinal rows of low warts. 25–30 mm. long at rest and 4–5 mm. in width. Very active.

76. *Haementeria costata* (Fr. Müller). (Family Glossiphoniidae.) Found in water with abundant plant life. Rare in north-west Europe and does not occur in Britain.

77. *Glossiphonia complanata* (L.). (Family Glossiphoniidae.) Found in standing and running water. Feeds on snails, worms, insect larvae. Very variable in colour, mostly green to brown. 2 dark longitudinal bands. 6 longitudinal rows of yellowish warts, which lie on every third body ring. 10–30 mm. long and 4–10 mm. wide. Does not swim. Common in running water and streams.

78. *Glossiphonia heteroclita* (L.). (Family Glossiphoniidae.) Found in ponds and slow-running water. Feeds on snails. Body smooth. Light yellow to greyish-white, sometimes covered with black spots. Up to 9·5 mm. in length and 5 mm. in width. Does not swim. Common.

79. *Helobdella stagnalis* L. (Family Glossiphoniidae.) Found in ponds and very sluggish rivers. Feeds on snails and worms. No pimples or markings. Often almost colourless, transparent; sometimes grey or reddish. Between the tenth and eleventh ring there are dark dorsal plates. 5–10 mm. long and 3–5 mm. wide. Common.

80. The medical leech. *Hirudo medicinalis* L. (Family Hirudinidae.) Chiefly found in moorland ponds and lakes. The young feed on invertebrates, later on fish, frogs and newts; the adults feed on mammals, including man. Back dark green with 6 reddish-yellow or brown longitudinal bands interrupted by black spots. Ventral side yellowish-green with irregular black spots. 10–15 cm. long and 1–1·5 cm. wide. Scattered throughout Britain.

81. The horse leech. *Haemopis sanguisuga* L. (Family Hirudinidae.) Found in still and running water. Devours smaller water-creatures of all types (worms, insect larvae, etc.). Back mostly brown, grey to black-brown with darker spots. Ventral surface yellowish-grey, with irregular black spots. Swims well. Common.

82. *Erpobdella octoculata* L. (Family Erpobdellidae.) Found in standing and running water. Eats small animals of very varied types. Very variable in colour, mostly brown with lighter spots. Up to 60 mm. long and 8 mm. wide. Able to roll itself up. Common.

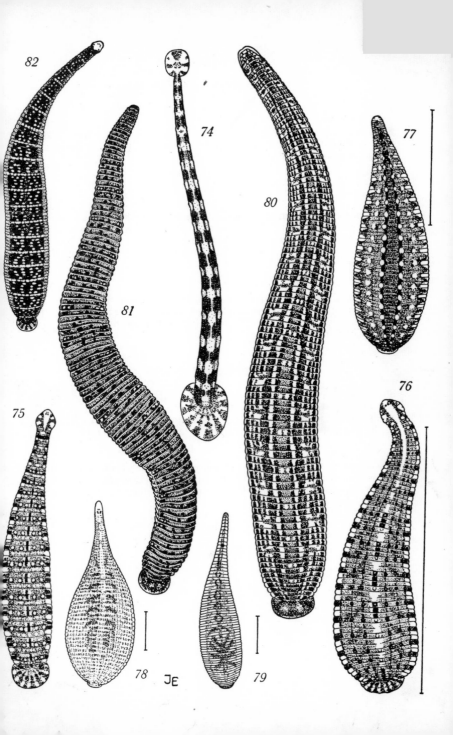

82

74

77

80

81

75

76

78   JE   79

CRUSTACEA

FAIRY SHRIMPS (*Euphyllopoda*)

(a) Notostraca

83. *Triops* (*Apus*) *cancriformis* Bosc. (Family Triopsidae.) Very rare in Britain. Found in shallow, muddy ponds from April to middle November. Brown in colour. Total length up to 10 cm.

(b) Anostraca

84. *Chirocephalus diaphanus* Prevost. (Family Branchipodidae.) The only British species, occasionally found in shallow, muddy pools in south and south-west England from May to September. Whitish in colour; sometimes pinkish or greenish. 11·5 mm. long. Often found in company with *Triops cancriformis*. Very rare.

85. *Artemia salina* L. (Family Branchipodidae.) Found in salt lakes and salt marshes on the Continent. Reddish in colour. 8–11 mm. long. The plate shows a ♀ from above. Now extinct in Britain, but artificially cultured as fish-food.

WATER-FLEAS (*Cladocera*)

86. *Scapholeberis mucronata* (O. F. Müller). ♀ (Family Daphnidae.) Widely distributed, and found close to the bank in standing water. Length of ♀ about 1 mm. and of ♂ 0·5–0·7 mm. Swims upside down close to the surface of the water. 1 other species found in Britain (*S. aurita*) is rare.

87. *Moina rectirostris* Leydig. ♀ (Family Daphnidae.) Principally found in pools with muddy bottom and in murky water in England and South Wales. Whitish-grey in colour. Length of ♀ 1–1·6 mm.; ♂ 0·8–1 mm. 2 other species in Britain.

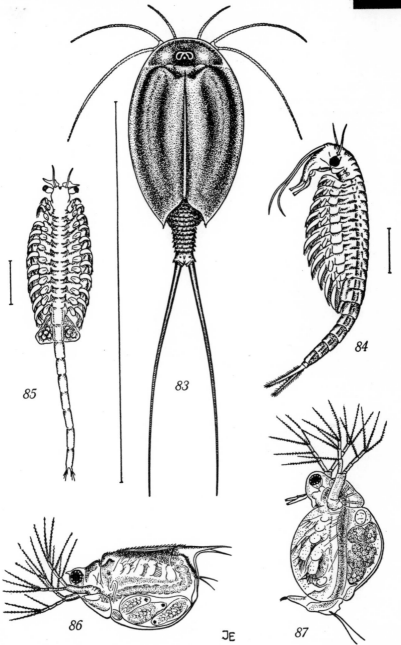

85   83   84

86   JE   87

88. Common water-flea. *Daphnia pulex* Degeer. ♀. (Family Daphnidae.) Found in pools and smaller or average-sized ponds. Transparent green, yellow or pinkish in colour. Length of ♀ 3–4 mm.; ♂ 1–1·5 mm. Common. 10 British species in the genus *Daphnia*, with many varieties.

89. *Simocephalus vetulus* O. F. Müller. ♀ (Family Daphnidae.) Found close to the banks in water with abundant plant life. Colour of ♀ dark green or brown, 2–3 mm. in length; ♂ 1 mm. It swims fast, often on its back. Clings to plants. Very common. 2 other species in Britain.

90. *Ceriodaphnia quadrangula* O. F. Müller. ♀ (Family Daphnidae.) Found in ponds and lakes and clear water. Length of ♀ 0·6–0·8 mm. and of ♂ 0·6 mm. Common. 7 other species in Britain.

91. *Sida cristallina* O. F. Müller. ♀ (Family Sididae.) Found close to the shore in standing water among plants. Very transparent. Length of ♀ 3–4 mm.; ♂ 2 mm. Clings to water-plants. Swims swiftly. Common; only 1 species.

92. *Bosmina longirostris* O. F. Müller. ♀ (Family Bosminidae.) Found in clear water along the banks of ponds and lakes and also in the plankton. Length of ♀ 0·4–0·6 mm.; ♂ 0·4 mm. Common. 1 other British species.

93. *Acantholeberis curvirostris* O. F. Müller. ♀ (Family Macrothricidae.) Chiefly found in moorland ponds. Green or greenish-yellow in colour. Length of ♀ 1–1·7 mm.; ♂ 0·7 mm. Only 1 species; widely distributed, but rather rare.

94. *Eurycercus lamellatus* O. F. Müller. ♀ (Family Chydoridae.) Found among weeds in ponds and lakes. Ventral edge of carapace almost straight. Length of ♀ up to 6 mm.; ♂ 1·3 mm. Swims well and clings to plants. Common. 1 other species, very rare, in Scotland.

95. *Chydorus sphaericus* O. F. Müller. ♀ (Family Chydoridae.) In nearly all still water. Commonest of all water-fleas. Colour very variable. Length of ♀ 0·3–0·5 mm.; ♂ 0·2–0·4 mm. 5 other species in Britain.

96. *Polyphemus pediculus* L. ♀ (Family Polyphemidae.) Found along the banks of ponds and lakes; more rarely among plankton; also in moorland water. Length of ♀ 1·4–1·6 mm.; ♂ 0·9 mm. Only 1 species, widely dispersed.

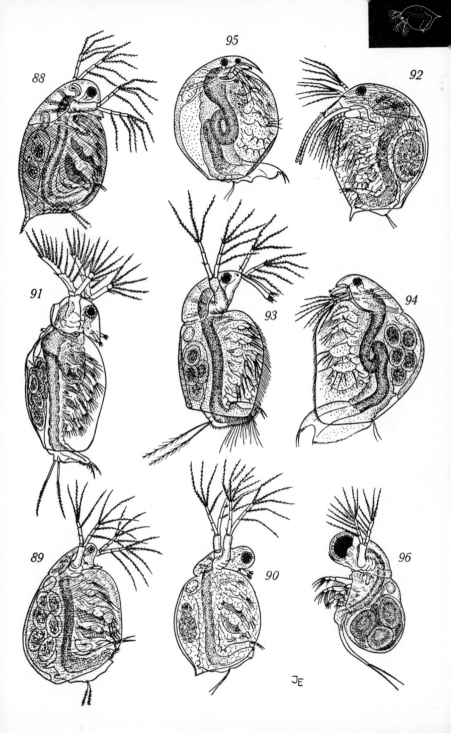

97. *Diaptomus* sp. ♀ (Family Centropagidae.) 6 species found in Britain, living in clear water in ponds and lakes. 1st antenna has 24–5 segments. ♀ has only 1 egg-sac. Length of the most common species: ♀ 2–4 mm.; ♂ 2–3 mm.

98. *Cyclops* sp. ♀ (Family Cyclopidae.) Many species. Colouring variable. Mostly found among plants in still water. 1st antenna with 8–17 segments ♀ has 2 egg-sacs. Length not more than 1 mm., most species being much smaller.

99. *Canthocamptus* sp. ♀ (Family Harpacticidae.) Numerous genera and species, all similar. Length of the most common species: ♀ 0·6–0·8 mm.; ♂ 0·4–0·6 mm. Short antennae, and the abdomen not clearly marked off from the thorax.

100. *Nauplius* larva of the *Copepoda*.

Ostracoda

Identification of the numerous native *Ostracoda* is based principally on the form of bristling on the limbs, and is extremely difficult and can only be undertaken by a specialist. There is therefore little point in giving further details here. Three of the most common species are illustrated as examples.

101. *Herpetocypris reptans* (Baird).

102. *Candona candida* (O. F. Müller).

103. *Notodromas monacha* (O. F. Müller).

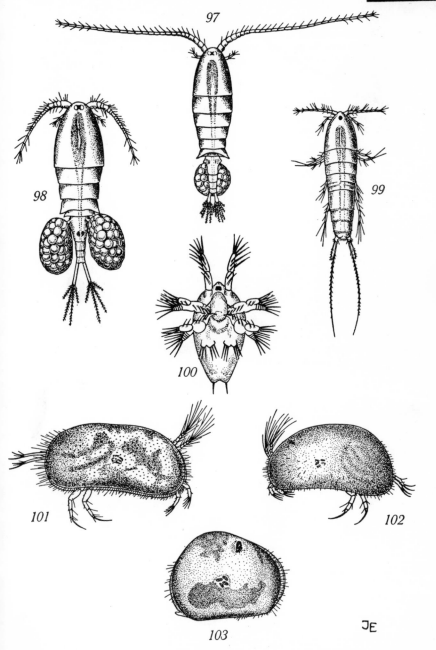

97

98

99

100

101

102

103

JE

WATER-LICE (*Isopoda*)

104. Water-louse. *Asellus aquaticus* L. (Family Asellidae.) Dirty grey-brown, sometimes pale violet in colour, with lighter patches. Eyes are present and clearly pigmented. Length: ♀ 8 mm.; ♂ 12 mm. Common and widely distributed throughout Britain.

105. *Asellus cavaticus* Schiödte. (Family Asellidae.) Found in wells, caves and underground streams in south England and South Wales. Whitish and transparent. Length, 5–8 mm. No eyes.

FRESHWATER SHRIMPS (*Amphipoda*)

106. Freshwater shrimp. *Gammarus pulex* (L.). (Family Gammaridae.) Found in running water. Whitish, greenish, yellowish in colour. Length of ♂ up to 20 mm.; ♀ about 15 mm. 4 other British species occur in brackish water.

107. *Carinogammarus roeselii* (Gervais). (Family Gammaridae.) Found in still water, especially on lake shores, under stones and in flowing water. Grey-brown to yellow-brown in colour. Length of ♂ up to 20 mm.; ♀ smaller. Found in Europe, but not in Britain.

108. *Niphargus* sp. (Family Gammaridae.) Found in wells, springs, caves and underground streams. Whitish and transparent. Length of ♂ up to 30 mm.; ♀ 10–18 mm. 4 species in south-west England.

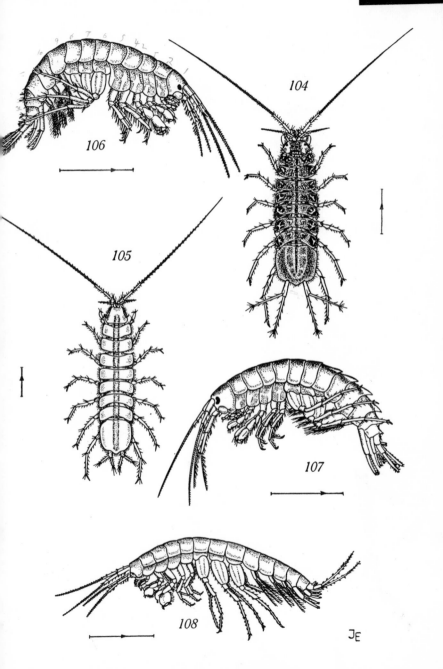

104

105

106

107

108

JE

ARACHNIDA

109. (1) The water-spider. *Argyroneta aquatica* (L.). (Family Argyrone-tidae.) Overall colour brown.

(2) The water-mites. *Hydracarina.* It is impossible to distinguish between the various native species of water-mites unless one has studied this group extensively and in great detail. Only 3 species are illustrated here to give some idea of the form of the whole animal. They are from 1 to a few mm. in size.

110. *Hydrodroma* sp.

111. *Unionicola* sp.

112. *Arrenurus* sp. ♂.

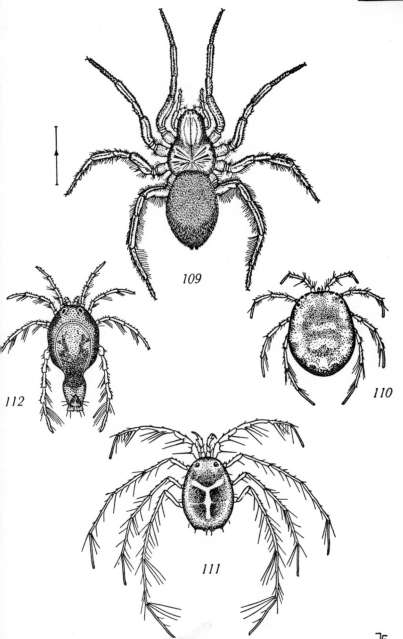

109

112

110

111

JE

INSECTA

Stone-flies (*Plecoptera*)

Identification of the species can only be made by an expert. In many cases even the identification of the genus is difficult. The main genera are listed.

113. Adult of *Nemoura* sp. (Family Nemouridae.) Brown. Length of body up to 10 mm. (excluding cerci). 4 genera and 11 species in Britain.

114. Small short-winged male of *Perla* sp. (Family Perlidae.) Brown with yellow markings. Length of body up to 20 mm. (excluding cerci).

115. *Perla* sp. Nymph. (Family Perlidae.) 2 species, mostly found in larger stretches of flowing water on stones. 16–21 mm. long (excluding cerci). Black, yellow or brownish-yellow. Markedly flattened. Tufted tracheal gills on both sides of all 3 thoracic segments. In some species there are additional gills at the posterior end between the cerci. 3rd tarsal joint much longer than the 1st and 2nd together. Predators.

116. *Isoperla* sp. Nymph. (Family Isoperlidae.) 2 species found in streams and rivers. Younger nymphs cling to water-plants and older ones to stones. About 10 mm. long (excluding cerci). Mostly variegated markings. Moderately flattened. 3rd segment of the maxillary palps shorter than 4th; the latter somewhat slimmer than the preceding one. Predators.

117. *Perlodes* sp. Nymph. (Family Perlodidae.) 3 species. Found in flowing water on stones. Up to 30 mm. long (excluding cerci). Greyish-brown to yellow. Moderately flattened. No tracheal gills. 3rd segment of the maxillary palps not shorter than 4th; the latter not pointed. 3rd tarsal joint much longer than 1st and 2nd together. Predators.

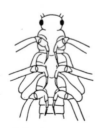

Ventral view of the thorax of *Taeniopteryx* sp.,
showing gills on the coxae

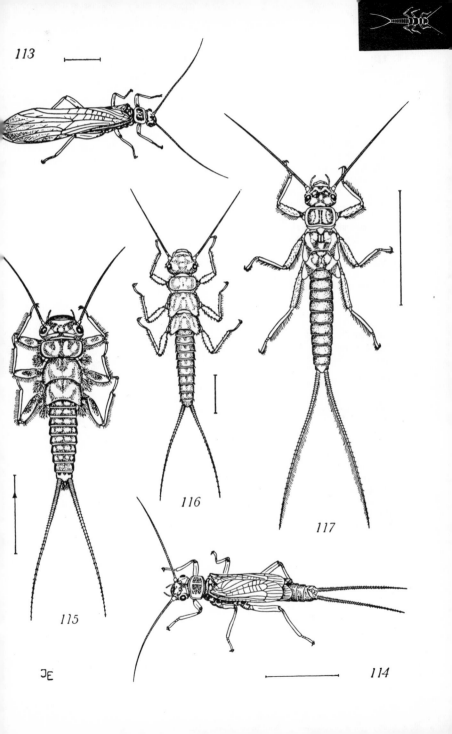

113

116

117

115

114

JE

118. *Chloroperla* sp. Nymph. (Family Chloroperlidae.) 3 species. Found in streams, mostly on stones. Up to 10 mm. long (excluding cerci); slim. Yellowish to reddish-brown. Notice the egg-shaped outline of the wing outgrowths. 4th segment of the maxillary palps knobby and thick; 5th segment markedly smaller and pointed. Hairs on the cerci longer than the corresponding segment. Feeds on detritus.

119. *Brachyptera* sp. Nymph. (Family Taeniopterygidae.) 2 species. Along the banks of streams. 8–10 mm. long (excluding cerci). Brown with lighter markings; lighter on the underside. Every tarsal joint longer than the preceding. Antennae and cerci very long; latter without hairs. Segments of the maxillary palps equally long. No gills. Feeds on detritus.

120. *Taeniopteryx nebulosa* (Linn.) Aubert. Nymph. (Family Taeniopterygidae.) As 119 above, but abdominal segments 1–7 have spines pointing rearwards. Underside, 3-part, filamentous, retractable gills on the inner side of each coxa (Figure 16).

121. *Nemoura* sp. Nymph. (Family Nemouridae.) 5 species in the genus; 11 species in the family. Very adaptable to widely differing conditions; found in all waters suitable for stone-flies, even the smallest watercourses. 6–9 mm. long (excluding cerci); sturdy, strong. Mostly dark brown. 2nd tarsal joint shorter than 1st and 3rd not much longer than 1st and 2nd together. 1st joint of the hind leg only about one-eighth as long as 3rd joint. The hind legs, when stretched out backwards, project beyond the end of the body. The 3 last segments of the maxillary palps are of equal length. The wing outgrowths slope outwards diagonally. No gills. Feeds on detritus.

Nemurella picteti Klapálek. Nymph. (Not illustrated.) (Family Nemouridae.) As No. 121, but 1st and 3rd segments of the hind leg are of equal length.

122. *Amphinemura* sp. Nymph. (Family Nemouridae.) 3 species in the genus. As 121, but on the underneath of the 1st thoracic segment on each side there are 2 tufts of tracheal gills. The number of gills increases with the age of the nymph up to 5 in the outer and 8 in the inner tuft (Figure 17).

Protonemura sp. Nymph. (Family Nemouridae.) 3 species. As 121, but on the underneath of the 1st thoracic segment there are 2 tufts with 3 sausage-shaped tracheal gills (Figure 18).

123. *Leuctra* sp. Nymph. (Family Leuctridae.) 6 species. Found in smaller stretches of water. 5–8 mm. long (excluding cerci); slim, yellowish. 2nd tarsal joint very short; 3rd joint of the foreleg at least 5 times as long as the 1st and 2nd together. The hind legs, when stretched out backwards, are about as long as the abdomen. Wing outgrowths parallel to the body. Feeds on detritus.

Ventral view of the prothorax of *Amphinemura* sp. with tufted gills

Ventral view of the prothorax of *Protonemura* sp. with tufted gills

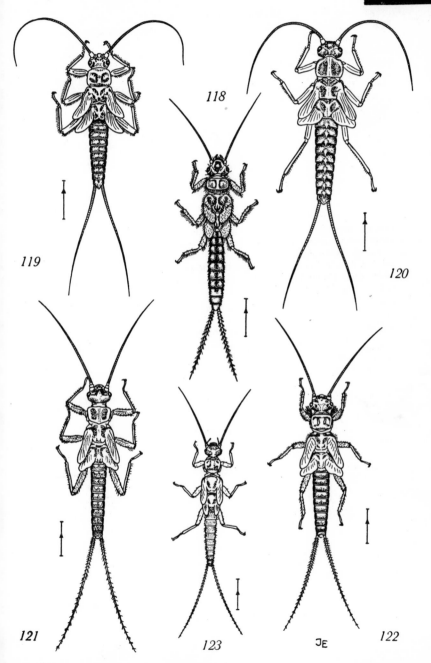

118

119

120

121

123

122

JE

124. *Ephemera vulgata* (L.). Nymph. (Family Ephemeridae.) Bury themselves along the banks of larger streams and lakes in U-shaped tunnels in the ground. Yellowish. 7 pairs of tracheal gills, which consist of double-branched, feather-like, fringed layers which lie across the back of the abdomen. The upper jaws are extended and spine-like and project in an outward curving arc beyond the head. 1 very similar and common species, *Ephemera danica* (Müll.). Length, 15–23 mm.

125. *Potamanthus luteus* (L.). Nymph. (Family Potamanthidae.) Found beneath and on stones in larger streams. Yellow with brown markings. 6 pairs of tracheal gills, which consist of double-branched, feather-like, fringed layers which project sideways from the abdomen. The upper jaws project considerably less than in 124, and each ends in 1 sharp tooth. Length, 10–12 mm. The only British species.

126. *Epeorus* sp. Nymph. (Family Ecdyonuridae.) Found in clear streams and smaller rivers with a high oxygen content in north-west Europe, but not in Britain. Yellowish with brown markings.

127. *Heptagenia* sp. Nymph. (Family Ecdyonuridae.) 4 species in flowing water and occasionally in clear lakes. Yellowish or grey-brown, with lighter markings. Body much flattened. Eyes situated on the top of the head. 7 pairs of tracheal gills, each consisting of 1 more or less pointed oval leaflet with a tuft of hairs beneath. Prothorax is rectangular, the posterior corners not extended. 9–14 mm. long.

128. *Ecdyonurus* sp. Nymph. (Family Ecdyonuridae.) 4 species in stony streams and rivers. Yellowish-brown to black with lighter markings. Shape and gills as 127. Gills more oval. The posterior corners of the prothorax are extended backwards over the mesothorax. Common and abundant. 8–15 mm. long.

129. *Rhithrogena* sp. Nymph. (Family Ecdyonuridae.) 2 species. Common in stony streams. Yellowish-green to greyish-green. Shape as 127. 7 pairs of lateral tracheal gills, consisting each of a leaflet with tuft of hairs beneath. Leaflets of 1st pair much enlarged and touching the abdomen. 8–12 mm. long (Figure 19).

Ventral view of *Rhithrogena* sp., showing the enlarged first pair of gills

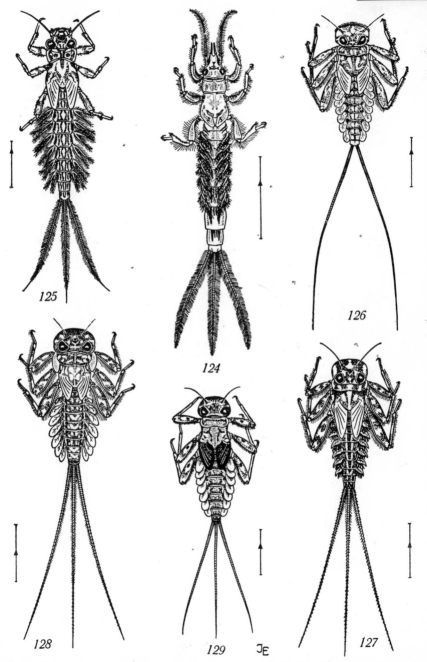

125

124

126

128

129 ᴊᴇ 127

130. Adult of *Ephemera vulgata* (L.). ♂ (Family Ephemeridae.) Length of body up to 20 mm. Wing length up to 17 mm. Tails, 30–5 mm. Whitish-brown.

131. *Ephemerella* sp. Nymph. (Family Ephemerellidae.) 2 species found in running water, often among water-plants. Yellow-brown. Body barely flattened. Eyes directed sideways. All tails bristled on both sides. 5 pairs of tracheal gills, which grow on the back on the posterior edge of the 3rd to 7th abdominal segment. The first 4 pairs of gills are visible; the 5th is hidden by the 4th. The 5th pair of gills does not have an ear-shaped lobe at the base. 7–10 mm. long.

132. *Chitonophora krieghoffi* Ulmer. Nymph. (Family Ephemerellidae.) Only 1 species in Germany; none in Britain. Found in flowing water. Brown with lighter markings.

133. *Torleya belgica* Lestage. Nymph. (Family Ephemerellidae.) Only 1 species in Germany; none in Britain. Found in flowing water and on stones covered with mud and algae.

134. *Caënis* sp. Nymph. (Family Caënidae.) 5 species. Found at the bottom of standing and running water. Yellow-brown. Body not flattened. Eyes directed sideways. All tails bristled on both sides, about half as long as the body. 6 pairs of gills on the 1st to 6th abdominal segments, but the 1st is very small and like a stalk; the 2nd is a large square plate, which covers all the subsequent gills. 2nd antennal segment not as long as the 3rd. 4–7 mm. long. Generally common.

    Brachycercus harrisella (Curtis). (Family Caënidae.) As *Caënis*, but 2nd antennal segment three times as long as 3rd. Three protuberances on the head. Rare.

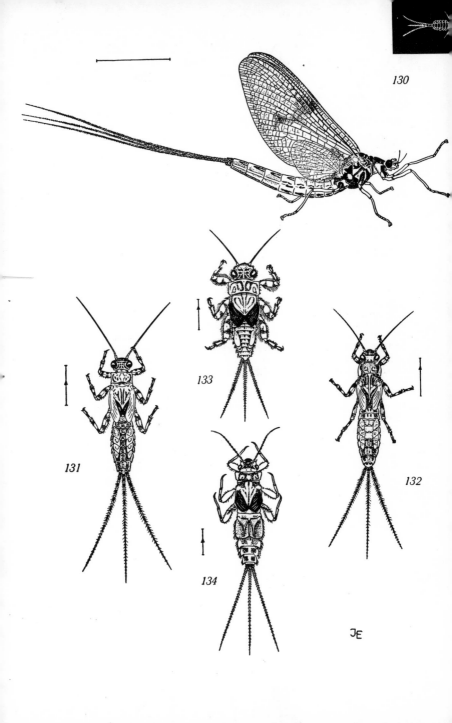

130

131

132

133

134

JE

135. *Siphlonurus* sp. Nymph. (Family Siphlonuridae.) 3 species. Chiefly found in dense weed in flowing water. Brownish with darker markings. Body narrow, not flattened. The last body segment elongated posteriorly into prongs. Head set like that of a grasshopper, vertical to the long axis of the body. The 2 outer tails with hairs only on the inside. 7 pairs of lateral, broad gills, the first 2 pairs double. 11–13 mm. long.

136. *Cloëon* sp. Nymph. (Family Baëtidae.) 2 species. Found in still and slow-flowing water. Swims well. Greenish with lighter markings. In shape similar to 135, but 7 pairs of gills, consisting of unequal parts, the first 6 pairs double, the 7th single. The posterior margins of the last abdominal segment not drawn out into a prong. 5–9 mm. long.

137. *Baëtis* sp. Nymph. (Family Baëtidae.) 9 species. Found in still and running water. Body narrow and not flattened. Head vertical to the long axis of the body. 7 pairs of lateral, oval, single gills, rounded at the end. 5–9·5 mm. long.

138. *Leptophlebia* sp. Nymph. (Family Leptophlebiidae.) 2 species found in still and running water. Yellowish-brown. Body very narrow. Head set vertically to the long axis of the body. 7 pairs of 2-part gills, the first feathery, the others basically leaf-shaped, running into fine pointed feathers. 7–12 mm. long.

139. *Habrophlebia fusca* (Curtis). Nymph. (Family Leptophlebiidae.) Found chiefly in slow-running water with much vegetation. Brown with blackish markings. In shape similar to 138, but 7 pairs of gills, much branched and all alike. 5–6 mm. long. Generally common.

140. *Habroleptoides modesta* (Hagen). Nymph. (Family Leptophlebiidae.) Found in streams. Yellow-brown with darker markings. Not found in Britain.

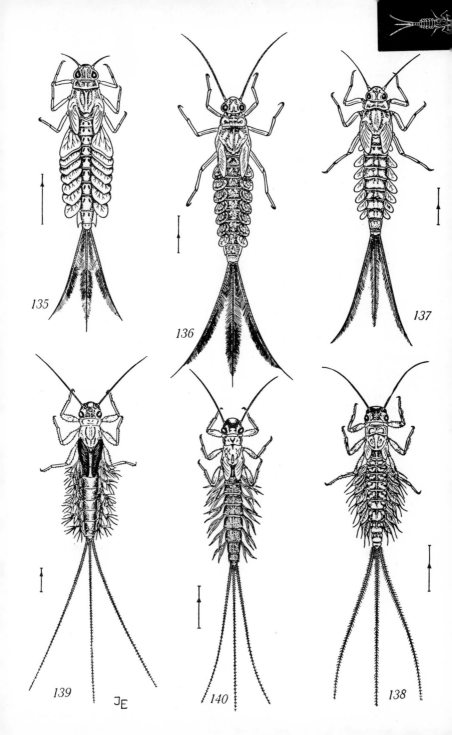

135

136

137

139

JE

140

138

POND-SKATERS (*Gerridae*)

141. Pond-skater. *Gerris* sp. (Family Gerridae.) 10 species. Mainly brown to black. Length (excluding legs) of smaller species, 5–9 mm.; of larger species, 12–17 mm. Widely distributed on still water.

142. Nymph of *Gerris* sp.

143. Water-gnat. *Hydrometra stagnorum* L. (Family Hydrometridae.) Part of head in front of eyes about twice as long as that behind them. Blackish. 9–12 mm. long. Common and widely distributed in vegetation at the edge of slow-moving water.

Hydrometra gracilenta Horv. (Family Hydrometridae.) Part of head in front of eyes only 1½ times as long as that behind them. Mostly light brown. 7·5–9 mm. long. Rare; only in Norfolk Broads.

144. *Velia caprai* Tamanini. (Family Veliidae.) Black. Ventral surface orange yellow, usually with a continuous black longitudinal band at the sides. 6–7 mm. long. Common. The other less common British species is *Velia saulii* Tamanini.

145. *Microvelia* sp. (Family Veliidae.) Mainly black. Antennae with 4 segments. 1st segment shorter than the head and straight; 4th segment the longest (cf. *Velia*). Adults about 2 mm. in length. 3 species. *M. reticulata* is common in reed-swamps.

146. *Mesovelia furcata* Muls. Rey. (Family Mesoveliidae.) Only 1 species. Greenish-brown; legs brownish-yellow. 3–3·5 mm. long. On floating leaves, especially *Potamogeton natans*, in south England. Not common.

147. *Naeogeus* (*Hebrus*) *pusillus* Fall. (Family Hebridae.) Black with reddish colouring on the head, thorax and ventral surface. Antennae with 5 segments, the last segment being shortest (a simple way of distinguishing it from *Microvelia*). Length, about 2 mm. Common in wet *Sphagnum* moss at the edge of small mountain ponds.

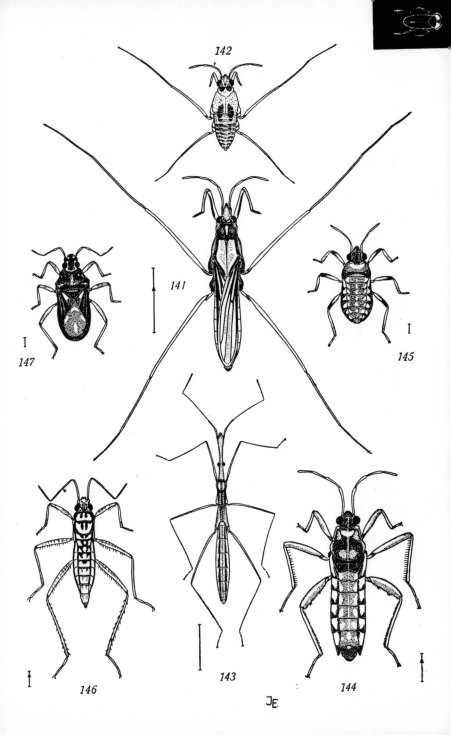

141

142

143

144

145

146

147

JE

Dytiscidae

148. Larva of the great diving beetle. *Dytiscus marginalis* L. About 50–60 mm. when fully grown.

149. *Hyphydrus ovatus* L. Very common in still water. Body on both sides almost spherically domed. Claws on hind feet unequal in length. Rust red. Elytra with darker markings. Front and middle tarsi apparently with 4 segments. 4·5–5 mm. in length.

150. *Hygrotus inaequalis* F. Common and widely distributed in standing water. Elytra very evenly and densely dotted. Rust-red with black patches, as shown in the plate. 2 equal claws. Front and middle tarsi apparently with 4 segments. 3 mm. long. 4 species of the genus in Britain.

151. *Hydroporus palustris* L. Common everywhere in standing water. Ventral surface black; dorsal surface black with yellow patches and stripes, as in plate. Fore and middle tarsi apparently with 4 segments. 3·5–4 mm. in length. 33 species in Britain.

152. *Coelambus impressopunctatus* Schall. Found in standing water in England and south-west Scotland. Domed. Rust-red. Elytra with 4 longitudinal stripes, tailing off at the posterior end and raised up by a double row of dots; coarse, densely dotted at posterior end. Ventral surface black. 2 side patches at the crown; the base of the thorax black in the centre. Longitudinal lines on the elytra black. Normal claws. Fore and middle tarsi apparently with 4 segments. 5 mm. long.

153. *Hydroporus pictus* F. Commonly found in still water. Body domed. Thorax and abdomen black. Head reddish-brown. Thorax black with lighter anterior and posterior edge and yellowish-red sides. Elytra yellowish-red with black markings, as in the plate. Fore and middle tarsi with 4 segments. 2–3 mm. long.

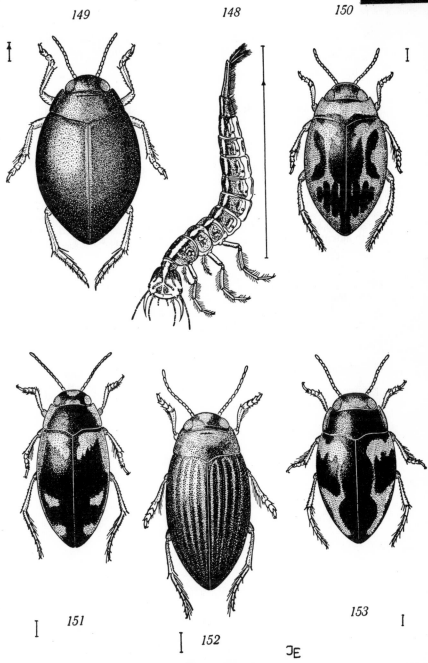

149

148

150

151

152

153

JE

Dytiscidae

154. *Agabus bipustulatus* L. ♀. Common everywhere in still water and bays in running water. Prefers cold, clear water. Segments of the hind feet cut off straight. Black, often with 2 reddish patches on the crown. Mouth, antennae and tips of legs rust-red. About 10 mm. long. 18 other species in Britain.

155. *Bidessus unistriatus* Schrank. ♀. Found in still water in south-east England. Recognisable by its 2 longitudinal folds, which run on either side from the base of the thorax to the base of the elytra. Domed. Head reddish-brown. Thorax reddish-yellow, often with a black hem on the posterior edge and often on the anterior edge too. Elytra dark brown with lighter and badly defined markings, dotted. 2 mm. long. 2 other species in Britain.

156. *Noterus clavicornis* (Degeer). ♂. Widespread in smaller ponds and pools. Body very much domed. Thorax and elytra with flattened edges. Head and thorax smooth. Elytra with coarse dots, largely arranged in rows. ♂ 5th antennal segment large, 6th just slightly smaller. 3·5–3·8 mm. long. 2 species in Britain.

157. *Laccophilus minutus* L. Found in still water. Lateral and anterior edge of the thorax smooth. Fore and middle tarsi with 5 segments. Greenish-brown with faded markings. 4·5 mm. long. 2 other species in Britain.

Haliplidae

158. *Haliplus fluviatilis* Aubé. Fairly common in rivers in England and south Scotland. Thorax trapezium-shaped, widest at the base. Black rows of dots on the elytra, with interrupted blackish lines. 2–3 mm. long. 16 species in Britain (*see* figure 21, p. 83).

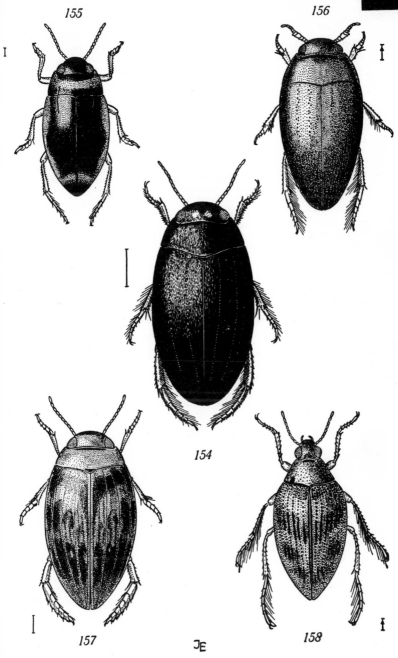

155

156

154

157

158

JE

159. Larva of the silver water-beetle. *Hydrous piceus* (L.). Black-brown. Length of fully grown larva, 70 mm.

160. *Hydrochara caraboides* (L.). In small ponds and pools. Black with pale greenish sheen, base of antennae and tarsal segments rust yellow. 14–18 mm. long. Local.

161. *Hydrobius fuscipes* L. Common in stagnant water. Black, usually with a pale bronze sheen. Legs rust-red with darker coxae. Elytra with rows of dots. Last segment of the palps longer than the penultimate. 6–7·5 mm. long.

162. *Enochrus affinis* Thunb. Found in still water. Yellow-brown. Head black, with red patches in front of the eyes. Legs rust-red, palps very long, last segment dark and shorter than the penultimate. 3–4 mm. long.

163. *Laccobius alutaceus* Thoms. Found in still and running water. Domed to form almost half a sphere. Yellowish-brown. Head and thorax black. Elytra densely dotted and striped, black, with flat areas between. Length, about 3 mm. 7 other species in Britain.

164. *Hydraena riparia* Kugel. ♀. Common in running water, mostly on stones, water-plants and wood. Palps very long, their last segment longer than the penultimate. Black. (Elytra sometimes brownish.) Legs and tarsal segments red, tips of the tarsal segments blackish. Regular thick rows of dots on the elytra. 2·2–2·4 mm. long. 9 other species in Britain.

161

160

162

163

159

164

JE

165. *Elmis aenea* Müll. Found in flowing water on stones and water-plants. 5 segments on feet, claw segment markedly long, club-shaped, longer than the 4 preceding segments together. Claws large. Gleaming black, elytra having a bronze sheen. Antennae and legs partially or all brownish-red. Body bald. 1·5–2·5 mm. long. Locally abundant.

166. Larva of *Elmis aenea* Müll. Dark brown. Length, 3–4 mm.

167. *Dryops* sp. (Family *Parnidae*.) Found along the banks of flowing and still water. Thorax on both sides has deeply indented longitudinal stripes with sharp outer edges. Body, including eyes, densely haired. Foot segments as 165, black or blackish-brown, the hairs in many species yellowish-grey. 4–5 mm. long. 7 species in Britain, 2 of which are common.

WHIRLIGIG BEETLES (*Gyrinidae*)

168. Hairy whirligig. *Orectochilus villosus* Müller. Common in running water. Dorsal surface densely and finely haired. Black. Hairs grey. 6 mm. long. Only 1 species in Britain.

169. Larva of whirligig beetle. Yellowish-white. When fully grown, about 12 mm. long.

WEEVILS (*Curculionidae*)

170. *Litodactylus leucogaster* Marsh. Found on water-plants, mostly *Myriophyllum* sp., under water. Body covered with water-repelling scales and always surrounded by a layer of air. Respiration probably as for *Dryopoidea*. Unable to swim. Light green with dark green patches. About 2 mm. long. About 40 species of this large family live on aquatic plants and spend most of their lives submerged.

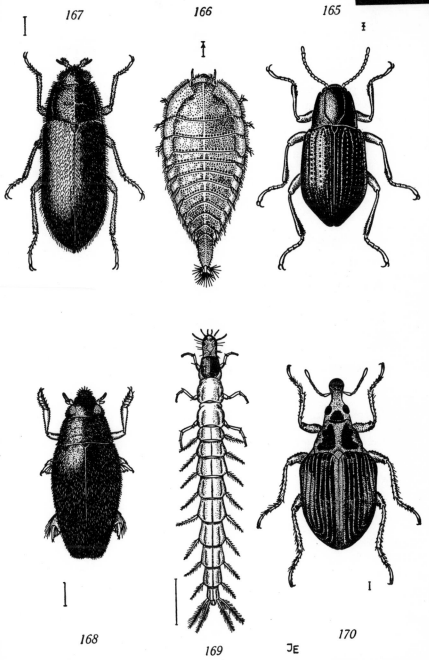

167

166

165

168

169

170

JE

PLATE 5

1. Water-stick-insect. *Ranatra linearis* L. (Family Nepidae.) 30–40 mm. long, excluding breathing tube. Locally common in southern England in still water with dense vegetation.

2. Water-scorpion. *Nepa cinerea* L. (Family Nepidae.) 17–22 mm. long, excluding breathing tube. Widely distributed, but seldom abundant. In shallow water with thick vegetation.

3. Water-boatmen. *Corixa* sp. (Family Corixidae.) Length, according to species, 5–15 mm. (32 species in 3 genera). The 3 *Micronecta* species belong to this family, and are very similar in overall characteristics to the *Corixa* species, but are only about 2 mm. long. Corixids are common in all types of water, though any one species is often characteristic of its habitat.

4. *Notonecta* sp. (Family Notonectidae.) Seen from above. 4 species in Britain. Widely distributed in ponds and lakes. 13–16 mm. long.

4a. *Notonecta* at rest, taking air supply.

5. *Plea leachi* MacGreg. (Family Notonectidae.) Abundant in thick vegetation in ponds in southern England. 2–3 mm. long.

6. *Ilyocoris cimicoides* L. (Family Naucoridae.) Widely distributed and fairly common, although seldom in large numbers. 12–16 mm. long.

7. *Aphelocheirus montadoni* Horv. (Family Aphelocheiridae.) 8·5–10 mm. long. Mostly in southern England and the Midlands. Locally common on stony bottoms in rivers.

PLATE 5

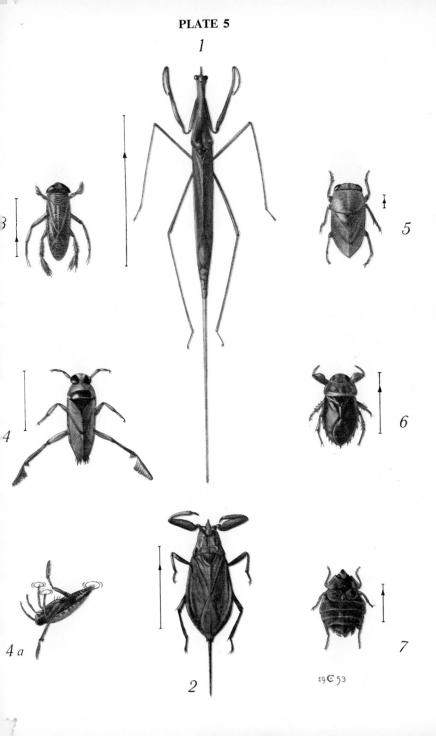

PLATE 6

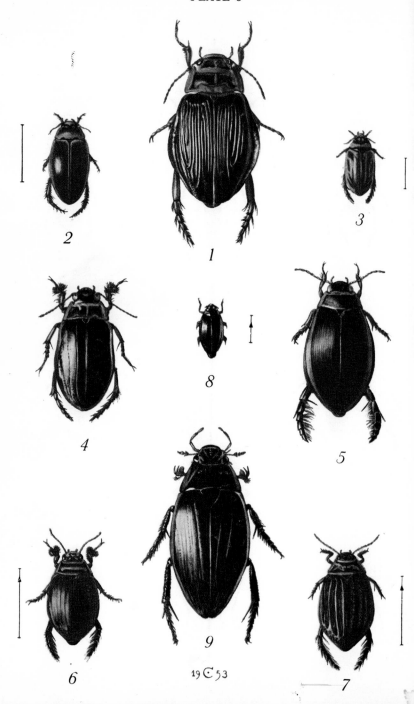

2

1

3

4

8

5

6

9

7

19 C 53

PLATE 6

BEETLES (*Coleoptera*)

Dytiscidae

1. *Dytiscus latissimus* L. ♀. Found in larger ponds and pools in north-west Europe, but not in Britain. Elytron with widely-spread flutes. 36–44 mm. long.

2. *Graphoderus cinereus* L. ♀. Found in still water. 15 mm. long. Very rare. East Anglia.

3. *Platambus maculatus* L. Common throughout Britain in running water; in weeds along banks of streams. The blackish-brown longitudinal stripes on the elytra vary in density, so that often almost yellow and practically black-brown animals occur. 8 mm. long.

4. Great diving beetle. *Dytiscus marginalis* L. ♂. Locally common in ponds and pools. Ventral surface almost or completely yellow. The continuation of the coxa of the hind legs is drawn out into a short point. (See Figure 20, page 81.) 30–5 mm. long.

5. *Cybister lateralimarginalis* Degeer. ♀. Very rare; found only 3 times in England in 1826–31. Found in ponds. Distinguished from *Dytiscus*, as hind tarsi have only 1 claw. 30–5 mm.

6. *Acilius sulcatus* L. ♂. Found in stagnant water, especially peat pools. Upper and lower surfaces very closely and strongly marked with dots. Thorax has 2 black transverse bands. 16–18 mm. long.

7. *Acilius sulcatus* L. ♀. As 6 above, but on the elytra 3–4 smooth longitudinal ribs, with thick hairs between.

WHIRLIGIG BEETLES (*Gyrinidae*)

8. *Gyrinus natator* L. Commonly found on the surface of stagnant water. Upper surface is bald. Elytra have 11 rows of dots, of which the inner are sometimes missing. 5–7 mm. long. 12 species in 3 genera of this family in Britain.

Hydrophilidae

9. Silver water-beetle. *Hydrous piceus* L. Found in larger ponds and pools. 34–7 mm. long. Southern England; very local.

Metacoxae of *Dytiscus marginalis*

The True Flies (*Diptera*)

MIDGES, MOSQUITOES AND CRANE-FLIES (*Nematocera*)

MIDGES (*Chironomidae*)

171. *Chironomus* sp. larva.

172. *Chironomus* sp. pupa.

173. *Chironomus* sp. adult ♂.

174. Puparium of the midge *Rheotanytarsus* sp.

Ceratopogonidae

175. Larva of *Bezzia* sp. Whitish-yellow.

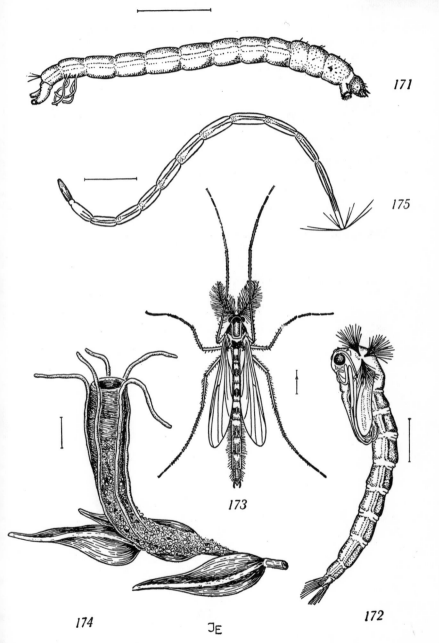

171

175

173

174

172

JE

176. Larva of *Culex* sp. Brown. Length, about 10 mm. Note the position, suspended from the surface of the water.

177. Pupa of *Culex* sp.

178. Larva of *Anopheles* sp. Green. Length, about 10 mm. Note the position, suspended from the surface of the water.

179. Pupa of *Anopheles* sp.

180. Adult of *Anopheles* sp. ♀. Fully fed. Wings spotted. Depicted in characteristic resting position. The genera *Culex* and *Anopheles* are very difficult to distinguish morphologically. When resting, the proboscis and the body of *Culex* are at an obtuse angle. The proboscis is bent towards the substratum and the body is parallel to it.

181. Larva of the phantom midge. *Chaoborus crystallinus* Degeer. Length, about 12–15 mm.

182. Pupa of *Chaoborus crystallinus*. Standing vertically in the water.

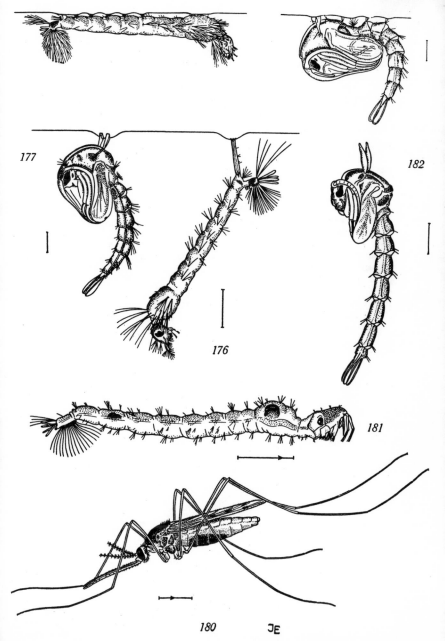

178

179

177

182

176

181

180   JE

183. Larva of the black-fly. *Simulium* sp. Brownish. Up to 15 mm. long.

184. Pupa of the black-fly. *Simulium* sp. Brownish, blackish brown before emerging. 6–10 mm. long.

185. Adult of the black-fly. *Simulium* sp. ♂ velvet black; ♀ grey. Length, 1·5–3 mm. About 15 species in Britain.

Dixa MIDGES (*Dixidae*)

186. Larva of the *Dixa* midge. *Dixa* sp. Yellowish or brownish grey with darker head and tail. Length, 6–10 mm. 13 species in Britain.

Blepharoceridae

187. Larva of *Liponeura* sp. Seen from above. Domed and grey. Ventral surface flat and whitish. Up to 9 mm. long. 2 species in Germany; none in Britain.

188. Pupa of *Liponeura* sp. Dorsal surface light to dark brown; ventral surface whitish. Length, 7–8 mm.

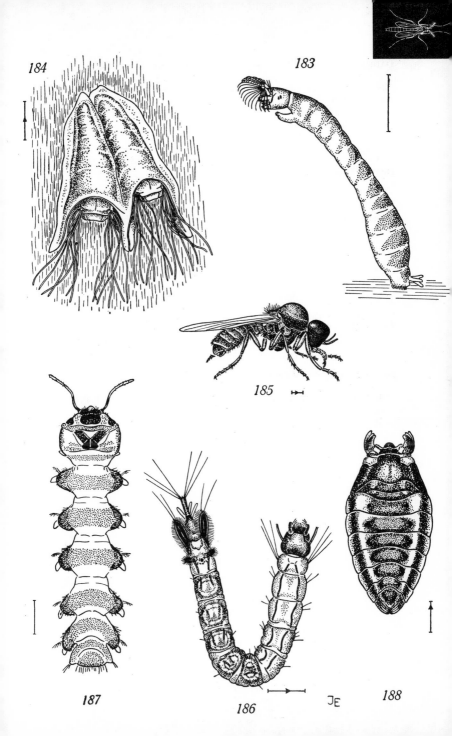

184

183

185

187

186

JE

188

189. Adult of the Crane-fly *Tipula* sp. ♂. Numerous species. Body light or dark brown. Wings variably marked. Length, excluding legs: smaller species, ♂ about 14 mm., ♀ about 20 mm.; larger species, ♂ about 20–25 mm., ♀ about 35 mm.

190. Larva of *Tipula* sp. Grey or yellowish. Head and spiracular plate dark brown. When stretched out, 30 mm. long and up to 10 mm. thick.

191. Larva of *Dicranota* sp. Dirty white, hairs black. Length, about 20 mm. Several species.

192. Larva of *Phalacrocera replicata* L. Green or brownish and about 30 mm.

Ptychopteridae

193. Larva of *Ptychoptera* sp. Whitish-yellow; transparent. When breathing tube is fully extended, up to 70 mm. long. 7 species in Britain.

MOTH-FLIES (*Psychodidae*)

194. Larva of *Psychoda* sp. White-grey. Length, about 1 cm. Several species have aquatic larvae.

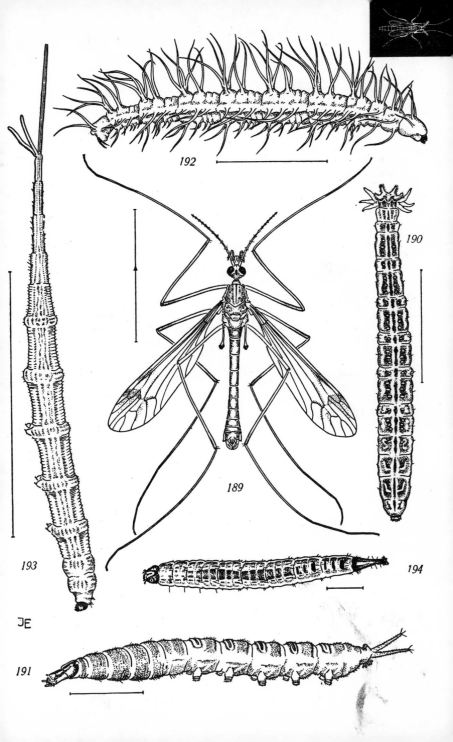

192

190

189

193

194

JE

191

HORSE-FLIES OR CLEGS (*Tabanidae*)

195. Larva of *Tabanus* sp. White or pale yellow. Length, 30–40 mm. Several species. The larvae are commonly found in streams among damp water moss and liverworts.

Stratiomyidae

196. Larva of *Stratiomys* sp. Greyish-green. Length, 40–50 mm. Several species.

HOVER-FLIES (*Syrphidae*)

197. Rat-tailed maggot. *Tubifera* (*Eristalis*) sp. Whitish-grey. Length, up to 20 mm. Breathing tube, up to 35 mm.

198. Adult of *Tubifera* sp. Several species. Mostly black and shiny or a dark metallic colour. Abdomen with bright yellow side patches. Wings transparent, often with brown markings. Length, according to species, 10–16 mm.

Ephydridae

199. Larva of *Ephydra* sp. 4 species. Grey or yellow-brown. Length when mature, 12–15 mm.

200. Pupa of *Ephydra* sp. Length, 8–10 mm.

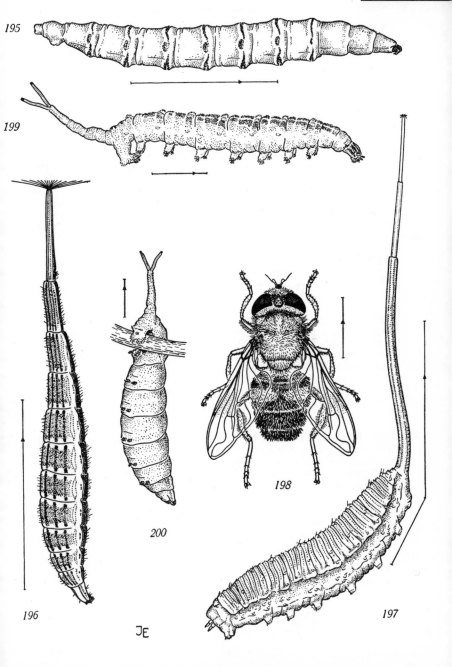

195

199

196

200

198

197

JE

Dragon-flies (*Odonata*)

Most dragon-fly larvae can only be identified by detailed morphological examination. Representatives of 9 genera are illustrated and these can be correctly identified at sight. At the same time, they present the basic types of 8 native families.

damsel-flies (*Zygoptera*)

These dragon-flies have 3 caudal gills.

201 Banded Agrion. *Agrion splendens* (Harris). Nymph. (Agriidae = Calopterygidae.) Principally found in flowing water among water-plants. Muddy yellow with blackish and whitish markings. Period of development lasting 2 years. Twice hibernates as larva. Length of body, 26 mm.; gills, 12 mm. First antennal segment very long and powerful, longer than the 6 others together. Outer gills have three edges, the centre one is shorter and leaf-shaped. Bumps on the back of the head behind the eyes are blunt and do not project above the eyes. See Figure 23, page 95.

Demoiselle Agrion. *A. virgo* (L.). Nymph. As above, but the bumps behind the eyes are pointed and project above the eyes. Centre gill is longer than in the case of *A. splendens*. See Figure 23.

202. *Lestes* sp. Nymph. (Family Lestidae.) 2 species of the family in Britain. Principally found in still water of all types. A few species also found in slow-flowing water. Basic colour, grey or yellowish-brown. Period of development, 8–10 weeks. Length of body, 15–20 mm.; gills, 8–10 mm. All caudal gills equal, flat with strong median veins from which the lateral veins run at right angles and lead without branching to the edge of the gill (Figure 23). Mask has a long base which, when resting, reaches right to the hind coxae.

203. White-legged damsel-fly. *Platycnemis pennipes* Pall. Nymph. (Platycnemididae.) Only 1 species found in ponds and lakes, chiefly on the bottom, or in slow-flowing streams among water-plants. Nymphs hibernate. Yellow or white with darker markings. Length of body, 19 mm.; gills, 7 mm. Caudal gills terminate in long spikes.

204. *Coenagrion* sp. Nymph. (Family Coenagriidae.) 12 species of the family in Britain. Principally found in still water among water-plants. Nymphs hibernate; green, yellow or greyish-brown, according to the species. Length varies according to species: body, 12–16 mm.; gills, 6 mm. Caudal gills have rounded ends or at the most short points. From the median vein the lateral veins branch off at acute angles (Figure 23).

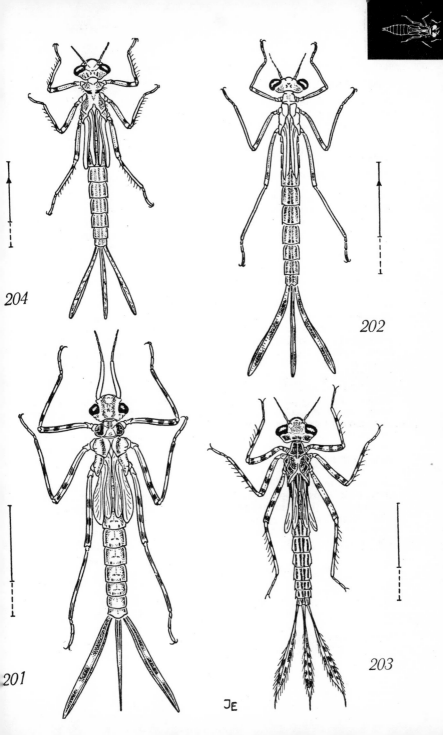

204

202

201

203

JE

At the posterior end of the body there is a pyramid of 5 projections.

205. Downy emerald. *Cordulia aenea* L. Nymph. (Corduliidae.) 4 species in Britain. Found in all types of still water, as well as in slow-flowing streams, usually on the bottom. Development varies with each species from 1–? years. Colouring differs according to species, as does length: body, 15–30 mm. Mask domed and helmet-like, the side lobes being evenly and slightly indented or wavy. Hind legs extend beyond the end of the body when stretched out backwards.

206. Golden-ringed dragon-fly. *Cordulegaster boltoni* (Donovan). Nymph. (Cordulegasteridae.) 1 species in Britain. Found in springs and mountain streams, buried in the mud, with only the eyes and tip of abdomen protruding. Probable period of development, 3–5 years. Brownish with black spots. Length over 40 mm. Head angular; eyes very small; mask domed and helmet-shaped, the inner edge of the side lobes being strongly and unevenly indented. Body densely covered with hairs. The hind legs, when extended, do not reach to the end of the body.

207. Club-tailed dragon-fly. *Gomphus vulgatissimus* L. Nymph. (Gomphidae.) The only British species. Found in running water or on muddy lake shores. It lies buried below the mud surface so that only the top of the head and the tail are visible. Period of development lasts 3–4 years. Yellow-brown. Length, 25–30 mm. Mask flat; when at rest does not extend backwards beyond the first pair of legs. Abdominal portion of the body flattened. Body covered densely with hairs.

208. *Aeshna* sp. Nymph. (Aeshnidae.) 7 species of the family in Britain. Mostly found in dense vegetation in still or slow-flowing water, at times also on the bottom. Development, according to species, 1–4 years. Green or dark brown. Mask flat, when at rest it reaches backwards at least to the 2nd pair of legs. Eyes large, body has no hairs. 6th to 9th abdominal segments with lateral projections.

209. Emperor dragon-fly. *Anax imperator* Leach. Nymph. (Aeshnidae.) Only found in weedy ponds and lakes. Development, 1 year. Basic colour greenish. Nymphs up to 60 mm. long. 7th to 9th abdominal segments with lateral projections.

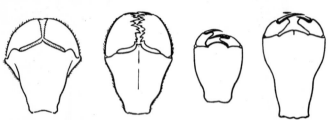

Masks (left to right): *Libellula* sp.; *Cordulegaster* sp.; *Gomphus* sp.; *Aeshna* sp.

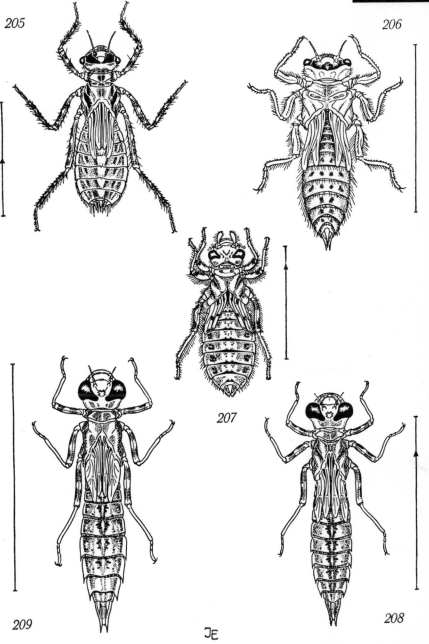

205

206

207

209

208

JE

ALDER-FLIES (*Megaloptera*)

210. Adult of the alder-fly (*Sialis* sp.). 3 species. Body black, wings brownish. Length, 25–30 mm.

211. Eggs laid by the alder-fly. Magnified 4 times.

212. Larva of the alder-fly (*Sialis* sp.). Whitish-yellow with dark to light brown markings. Gills whitish. Length, up to 40 mm.

LACE-WINGS (*Neuroptera*)

213. Larva of the sponge-fly. *Sisyra* sp. Green. Length, about 10 mm.

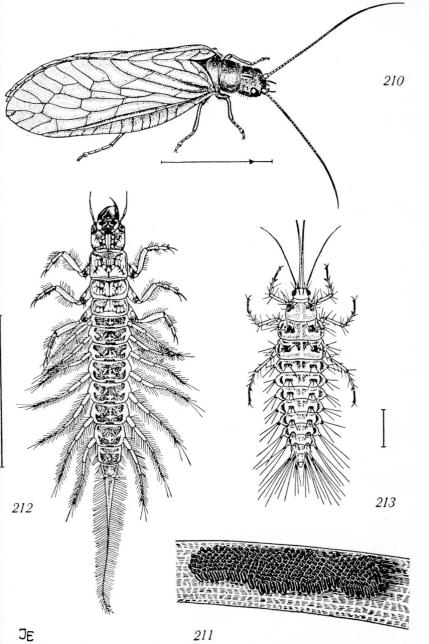

210

212

213

211

JE

PLATE 7

1. *Leucorrhinia pectoralis* Charp. ♂ (Libellulidae.) Found in Europe in peat ponds on plains but not in Britain. Length, 4·5–5 cm. Wing span, about 6·5 cm. On the wing from the beginning of May to the end of July. The only British species is the white-faced dragon-fly (*L. dubia*).

2. *Sympetrum pedemontanum* Allioni. ♂ (Libellulidae.) Found in Europe (but not in Britain) close to still water, above damp meadows, etc., but not over clear water. ♀ thorax greyish-brown, abdomen yellowish-brown. July to October. Related red-coloured species in England are *S. sanguineum* and *S. striolatum*.

3. Golden-ringed dragon-fly. *Cordulegaster boltoni* (Donovan). ♂ (Cordulegasteridae.) Found over springs and streams. Hunts over forest meadows and paths, etc. Length, 7–8·5 cm. Wing span, 9–10·5 cm. May to July.

4. Banded Agrion. *Agrion splendens* (Harris). ♂ (Agriidae.) Found over flowing water. ♀ body shining green with copper sheen at the end, its wings without bands and glass-like, through which metallic green veins show. Length, about 5 cm. Wing span, about 7 cm. May to September.

Closely related Demoiselle Agrion. *Agrion virgo* (L.). ♂ wings evenly dark brown with a blue sheen. ♀ wings dull greyish-brown. April to September.

5. Downy emerald. *Cordulia aenea* L. ♂ (Libellulidae.) Found over all types of still water. Hunts also on the outskirts of woods and in woods at dusk. Length, 5–5·5 cm. Wing span, 6·5–7·5 cm. May to August.

PLATE 7

1

2

3

4

5

PLATE 8

1. *Orthetrum brunneum* Fonsc. ♂ (Libellulidae.) Chief area around the Mediterranean and Near East; the 2 British species of *Orthetrum*, *O. cancellatum* and *O. coerulescens*, have the same coloration. Length, 4·5 cm. Wing span, 7–7·5 cm. June to August.

2. *Ophiogomphus serpentinus* Charp. ♀ (Gomphidae.) Found in Europe, but not in Britain, over flowing water with sandy bottom. Length, 5 cm. Wing span, 6·5–7·5 cm. June to October.

3. *Nehalennia speciosa* Charp. ♂ (Agrionidae.) Found in north-west Europe, but not in Britain, on high moors with fescue grass. Length, ⌐ ·2·5 cm., with a wing span of about 2·5 cm. July to August.

4. *Somatochlora flavomaculata* v.d.L. ♀ (Libellulidae.) Not a British species, but found in Europe over damp meadows and swamps, on the edge of woods and over woodland paths; not over open water. 2 yellow side spots on the forehead. Thorax metallic green and shimmering. Abdomen blackish-green with lateral yellow spots (in the case of older animals, brown). ♀ yellow spots on the abdomen markedly larger than those of ♂. Length, 5–5·5 cm. Wing span, 6·5–7 cm. May to August.

5. *Aeshna viridis* Eversin. ♂ (Aeshnidae.) European, but not British. Only 1 diagonal black stripe on the forehead. ♀ eyes olive green above and yellow below, abdomen reddish-brown and green. Length, 6·5–7·5 cm. Wing span, 8–9·5 cm. July to September. Similar British species is *A. juncea* L., the common aeshna. The costa (leading edge of wing) is yellow; divided blue spots on 9th and 10th abdominal segments. Yellow stripes on face and sides of thorax.

172

PLATE 8

1

2

3

4

5

19 C 53

PLATE 9

1. *Aeshna affinis* v.d.L. ♂ (Aeshnidae.) Found above marsh meadows and ditches; not over open water. A southern European species which has been occasionally recorded in Sussex as a summer migrant. ♀ patches on abdomen light yellowish-green. Length, 6–6·5 cm. Wing span, 8–8·5 cm. July to August.

2. Emperor dragon-fly. *Anax imperator* Leach. ♂ (Aeshnidae.) Found over ponds as well as considerable distances from any water. Light blue diagonal stripe on the top of the forehead. ♀ blue-green abdomen and markings broader and reddish-brown. Length, 7–8 cm. Wing span, 9·5–11 cm. June to August.

3. Green Lestes. *Lestes sponsa* (Hansemann). ♀ (Lestidae.) Found largely over still water of all types, as well as some distance from water. Length, 3·5–4 cm. Wing span, 4·5–5 cm. June to October.

4. White-legged damsel-fly. *Platycnemis pennipes* Pall. ♂ (Platycnemididae.) Found over still lakes and running water. Head blackish with 1 fine light blue transverse line on the front and back edge of the eyes. ♀ basic colour muddy yellow or pale green. Length, 3·5 cm. Wing span, 4·5 cm. May to September.

5. Large red damsel-fly. *Pyrrhosoma nymphula* Sulz. ♀ (Agrionidae.) Over slow-flowing water and also on occasions over still water. Length, about 3·5 cm. wing span, 4·5 cm. April to August.

6. Common Coenagrion. *Coenagrion puella* L. ♂ (Coenagriidae.) Found over wet meadows, still and slow-flowing water. ♀ abdomen laterally yellowish green or blue; the black markings cover almost the entire back. Length, about 3·5 cm. Wing span, 4–5 cm. May to September.

PLATE 9

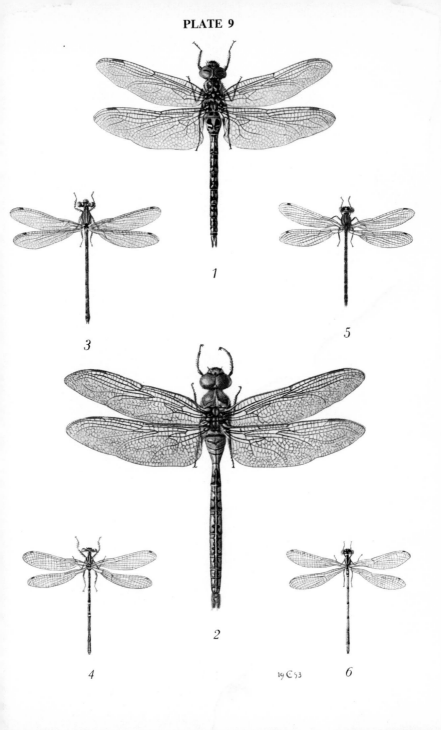

1

3

5

2

4

19 C 53

6

Aquatic Moths (*Lepidoptera*)

214. China mark moth. Adult of *Nymphula nymphaeata* L. (Family Pyralidae.) Body whitish (♀), brownish (♂). Wings white. Markings brown. Wing span, 21–6 mm. On the wing from June to August.

215. Larva of *Nymphula nymphaeata* L. in case.

216. Larva of *Nymphula nymphaeata* L. without case. Young: green; mature: light olive-brown with darker indentations and 3 dark longitudinal lines. Head and thorax olive-brown, shining. Length up to 25 mm.

Parasitic Wasps (*Hymenoptera*)

217. *Agriotypus armatus* Curtis. (Family Ichneumonidae.) Black. Length, about 10 mm. On the wing from the end of April to the middle of May.

218. Larval case of the caddis-fly (*Silo* sp.). The band shows that it is inhabited by the pupa of *Agriotypus armatus*.

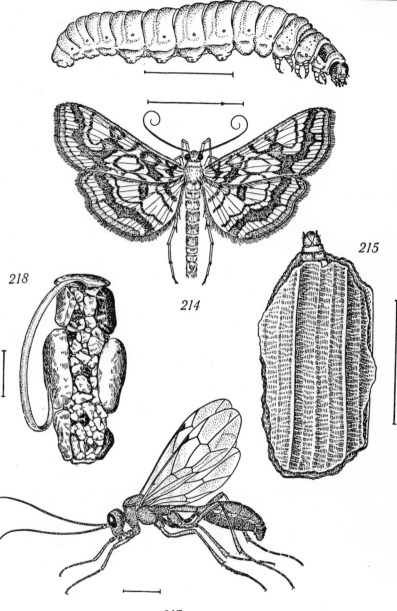

216

214

218

215

217   JE

The identification of caddis-fly larvae solely on the construction of the case is only possible in a few exceptional cases. In most cases identification demands the use of a microscope. A small selection of our most common native forms is illustrated. This should enable you to determine whether you have a caddis-fly larva before you.

219. Larva of *Rhyacophila* sp. (Family Rhyacophilidae.) 4 species in Britain. Campodeid. Found in swift-flowing streams with a stony bottom, principally in mountains. Lives free and does not construct a case or shelter. Basic colour yellowish with darker markings. Only the first thoracic segment (pronotum) is horny. Length of most species, up to 25 mm.

220. Larva of *Hydropsyche* sp. (Family Hydropsychidae.) 7 species in Britain. Campodeid. In the swiftly-flowing mountain streams and on plains. No case. Weaves fairly irregular shelters, in which areas of net with regular mesh can be set to catch food (Figure 24). All 3 thoracic segments horny, mostly grey-brown, square plates. Basic colour of the body yellowish; hairs black. Branched tufts of gills. Head with lighter patches, the posterior section of the body over its whole length about equally broad. 4 anal blood gills. Length, up to 20 mm.

221. Larva of *Plectrocnemia* sp. (Family Polycentropidae.) 3 species in Britain. Campodeid. Principally found in mountain streams. No case. Builds flat, conical-shaped webs. Only first thoracic segment horny, and this and head is light or dark brown. Abdomen reddish. No gills. Length, up to 22 mm.

222. Larva of *Ptilocolepus granulatus* Pict. (Family Hydroptilidae.) 1 species in north-west Europe. Not found in Britain. Lives in moss in springs and mountain streams. Case flat and made of small pieces of mossy leaves. Length, 8 mm.; width, 2 mm. Larva about 6 mm. long and 1·5–2 mm. wide. Head and thorax yellow-brown.

223. Larva of *Hydroptila* sp. With case. (Family Hydroptilidae.) 11 species in Britain. Campodeid. Found in still and flowing water. Case made of sand grains, pressed together at the sides and open front and back, carried on one edge.

223a. Larva of *Hydroptila* sp. Removed from its case. Note the lateral compression of the body. Length, 3–4 mm.; about 1 mm. broad.

224a–c. Larva of *Agapetus* sp. (Family Rhyacophilidae.) 3 species in Britain. Campodeid. Found in streams and small rivers. Case mostly made of larger sand grains. Length about 8 mm. and width 5 mm. (*a*) Case seen from above. (*b*) Seen from below, one can see the head and the legs of the larva at the top and below, the posterior end of the body and the caudal disc peeping out from the corresponding opening. Both openings face downwards and are surrounded by small sand grains. (*c*) Seen from the side.

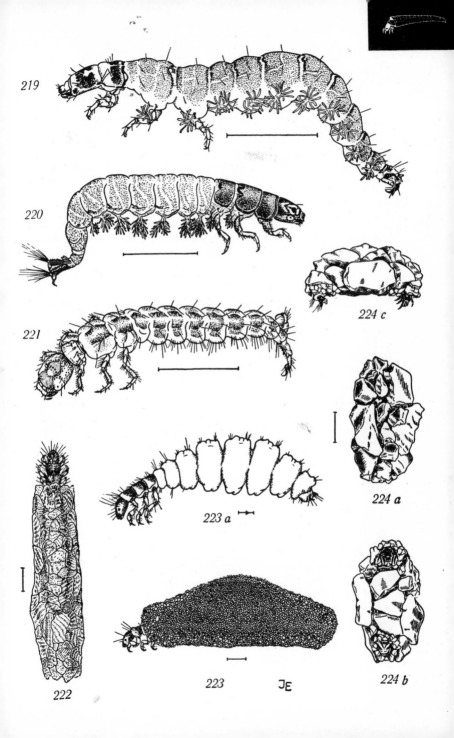

219

220

221

224 c

224 a

222

223 a

224 b

223   JE

225–8 show larvae of the *Limnephilidae*, the most extensive family of caddis-flies. There are 17 genera in Britain, of which the main genus, *Limnephilus*, alone has 25 species. The larvae inhabit all types of water; those without gills prefer flowing water and those with many gills select standing water. Characteristics of the family: Eruciform larvae with transportable cylindrical cases of varying shape. 1st and 2nd thoracic segments each with 1 square horny shield, divided down the centre by a line. 3rd thoracic segment has 3 pairs of chitinous plates. The top of the head usually has wedge-shaped markings, often with an X-shaped one in the centre of the posterior edge of the 1st thoracic segment, in the anterior third of which there is often a transverse furrow. Front legs shorter and stronger than the middle and hind legs. Middle legs stronger and longer than the hind legs. Underneath the thorax there is 1 horn-like appendage. A fine strip of hairs on each side of the abdomen.

225. Larva of *Limnephilus flavicornis* Fab. Found in the spring in still and slow-flowing water of all types. Case about 30–5 mm. long and 10 mm. wide.

226. Larva of *Limnephilus* sp. Case removed to show the abdomen, with lateral line and arrangement of gills. On the 3rd thoracic segment 3 chitinous plates can be clearly seen on the right side.

227. Larva of *Stenophylax* sp. Found in streams. Case: length, about 25–30 mm.; width, about 8–10 mm.

228. Larva of *Anabolia nervosa* Curt. Found in slow-flowing water and lakes. On top of the yellow head there is a mushroom-shaped black marking between the eyes and in front of this and on each side there is a crescent-shaped spot; on the back of the head there are rows of black dots (Figure 25, page 101). Case, 3–4 cm.; supporting parts often much longer.

229. Larva of *Silo* sp. (Family Sericostomatidae.) Found in swift-flowing streams on sandy or stony bottom. Case: length, 10–12 mm.; width, about 3 mm. (without side supports).

230. Larva of *Lepidostoma hirtum* F. (Family Sericostomatidae.) 2 species. Eruciform. Found in dense vegetation in flowing water. 1st and 2nd thoracic segments completely horny. 3rd thoracic segment with 3 pairs of small chitinous plates, of which the lateral pair is the largest and the central pair the smallest (Figure 25). Case of the young larva is a smooth, conical, straight sand tube; the older larval case, as illustrated, is made of leaf particles and is 4-sided. Length, up to 18 mm.; width, 2–3 mm.

231. Larva of *Sericostoma personatum* Spence. (Family Sericostomatidae.) The only species in Britain. Eruciform. Found in fast-flowing streams. Case made of sand grains. Length, up to 15 mm.; width, 2–3 mm.

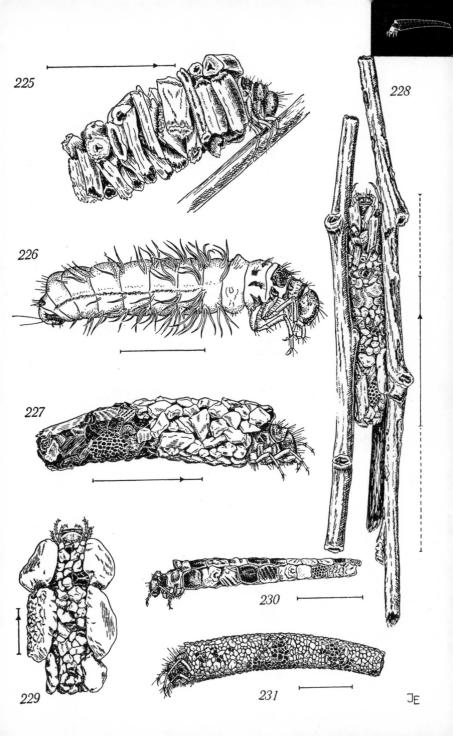

225

226

227

228

229

230

231

JE

232. Adult caddis-fly (*Phryganea* sp.).

233. Larva of *Phryganea* sp. (Family Phryganeidae.) 4 species in Britain. Found in standing water with dense vegetation. The Phryganeid larvae are sub-eruciform. Head and body axis form together an obtuse angle. 2nd and 3rd thoracic segments usually with soft skin. Chitinous appendage to the lower side of the 1st thoracic segment, well-formed lateral lines. 1st segment of the abdomen with 3 erectile warts. The rear lateral gills have fluffy hairs; all others smooth. Case almost always straight and open at both ends, mostly of spirally-arranged particles of plants. Case up to more than 50 mm. long and 10 mm. wide.

234. Larva of *Neuronia* sp. (Family Phryganeidae.) 2 species in Britain. Case removed.

235. Larva of *Triaenodes* sp. (Family Leptoceridae.) 3 species in Britain. Free-swimming in stagnant or slow-flowing water. Hind legs with long bristles for swimming. Case 20–30 mm. long, 2–3 mm. wide.

236. Larva of *Leptocerus* sp. (Family Leptoceridae.) 12 species in Britain. Mostly found in standing water with dense vegetation. Gills in tufts. Case from secretion and plant particles. Length, 12–15 mm.; width, 2–3 mm.

237. Larva of *Leptocerus* sp. Case removed. Gills only on 1st–3rd abdominal segments.

238. Case of *Molanna* sp. (Family Molannidae.) 2 species in Britain. Principally found in stagnant water with stony bottom. Case made of sand grains and has characteristic wings. Length, 15–25 mm.; width, 12 mm.

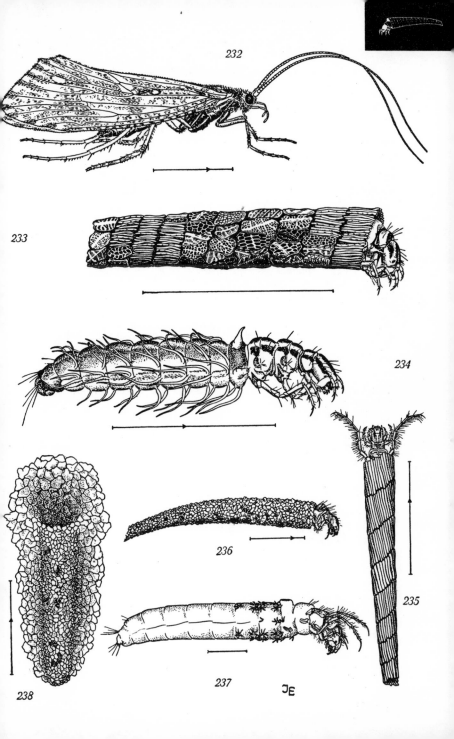

232

233

234

235

236

237

238

JE

Freshwater Snails, Limpets and Mussels (*Mollusca*)

MUSSELS AND COCKLES (*Lamellibranchiata*)

FRESHWATER MUSSELS (*Unionidae*). Shape of shell more or less long.

239. Swan mussel. *Anodonta cygnea* L. 2 species in central Europe. Found in ponds, lakes and slow-flowing rivers. No hinge-line teeth. Shell has thin walls, elongated oval in shape, posterior upper edge mostly raised to form a wing. Umbo little inflated, somewhat wrinkled and somewhat corroded. Brownish-green. Length, up to 200 mm. Numerous local forms.

240. Pearl mussel. *Margaritifer margaritifera* L. Found in fast-flowing rivers in north-west England and Ireland and Scotland with clean water and a low lime content. Hinge line having only cardinal and not lateral teeth. Shell with thick wall and heavy, umbo barely projecting, almost always corroded. Rust-brown to pitch-black, fairly matt. Mother-of-pearl bluish-white. Length, up to 120 mm.

241. Freshwater mussel. *Unio crassus* Retz. Not found in Britain. Lives in streams and rivers. Hinge-line with cardinal and lateral teeth. Right shell valve having 1 cardinal tooth and 1 long, sharp, wedge-shaped lateral tooth under the hinge-line. Left shell valve with 2 cardinal and 2 lateral teeth. Umbo fairly inflated. Thick walls to shell, oval, short, barely twice as long as it is high. Dark brown to black. Length, up to 60 mm.

242. *Unio timidus* Retz. Found in mud at the bottom of rivers and canals and lakes. Likes calm water. As 241, above, but umbo inflated, shell wedge-shaped and about twice as long as it is high, often with radial greenish stripes. 65–90 mm. long. Found in England and Wales only.

243. *Unio pictorum* L. In still and flowing water and in ponds. Characteristics as 241, above, but umbo inflated, shell valves narrow and tongue-shaped. Upper and lower edge almost parallel, more than twice as long as high. Yellowish-green with dark growth rings. Length, 70–100 mm. Found in England and Wales only.

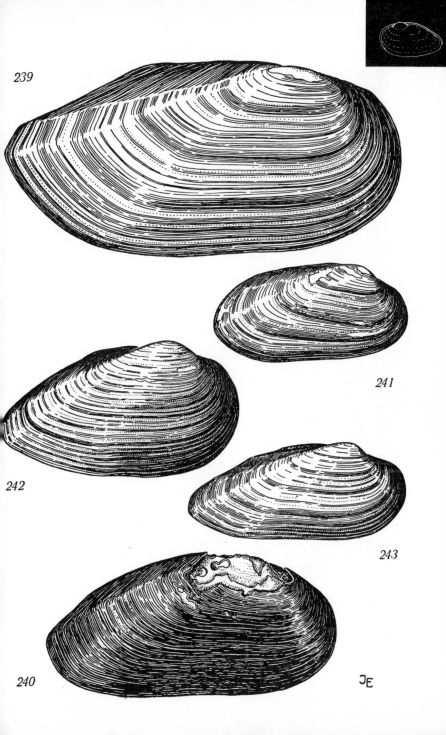

239

241

242

243

240

JE

FRESHWATER COCKLES (*Sphaeriidae*). More or less rounded shells.

244. Orb-shell cockle. *Sphaerium* sp. 4 species in Britain, of which *S. corneum* is much the commonest. Found in standing and slow-flowing water with gravelly bottoms. Both valves have almost equal sides. Umbo in the centre, only slightly projecting. Yellowish- or grey-brown. Length, up to 20 mm. 2 siphons.

245. *Musculium lacustre* Müller. 1 species in Central Europe; none in Britain. Lives in ponds and ditches. Shape as 244, but umbo tube-shaped with a cap consisting of the embryonal shell. Length and width up to 8 mm.

246. Pea-shell cockle. *Pisidium* sp. 15 species in Britain. Found in standing and flowing water. Many species in the deep regions of lakes. Shell valves unequal. Anterior end elongated, posterior shortened. Whitish-yellow, horn-coloured or brown. Length mostly under 10 mm. Only 1 siphon.

FRESHWATER MUSSELS (*Dreissenidae*)

247. *Dreissena polymorpha* Pall. Left and right shell valve. 1 species found in rivers and lakes, also old river beds. It clings to freshwater mussels, stones and posts, etc., by means of chitinous threads of a sticky quality from the byssus. Yellowish-green with brown wavy zigzag lines. Height, 15–18 mm.; length, 30–40 mm.; width, 20–5 mm.

SNAILS (*Gastropoda*)

Neritidae

248*a***.** *Theodoxus danubialis* C. Pfr. Found in the River Danube, but not in Britain. Outer edge of the operculum without a red fringe. Colour of shell yellow-grey with dark zigzag lines. Height, 9–10 mm.; width, 6–8 mm.; length, 11–13 mm.

248*b***.** *Theodoxus danubialis* C. Pfr. Underside. Note the operculum. The British species, *Th. fluviatilis*, the Nerite (not illustrated), has the outer edge of the operculum with red fringe. Colour of shell whitish with light or dark red (sometimes violet) interlocking markings. Size approximately the same as 248*a*. Fairly common in calcareous rivers.

FRESHWATER LIMPETS (*Ancylidae*)

249. River limpet. *Ancylastrum fluviatile* Müller. Seen from the side. Very common in lakes, ponds, rivers and streams. Often in very fast-flowing water. Shell form varies according to location. Height, up to 4 mm.; length, 5–7 mm.; width, 4–5 mm.

250. Lake limpet. *Ancylus lacustris* L. Sits on plant stems and leaves in still and stagnant water, often on the undersides of water-lily leaves. Soft body very much smaller than the flat shell, which shelters it like a roof. Height, 2 mm.; length, 7 mm.; width, 3 mm.

250*a***.** Outline of shell of *Ancylus lacustris* from the side.

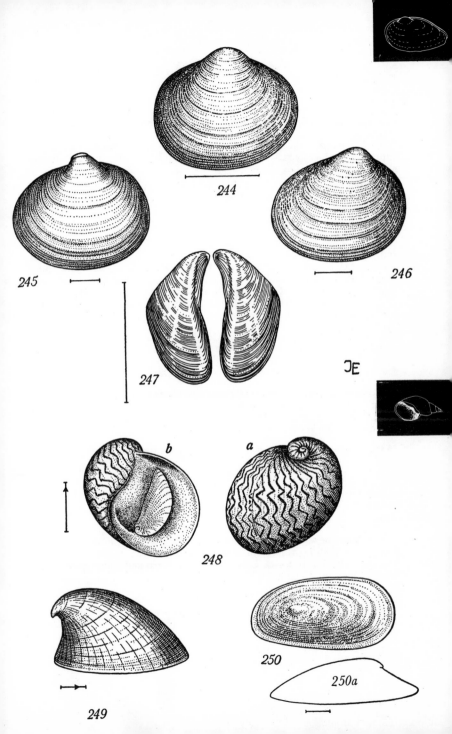

244

245

246

247

b *a*

248

249

250

250a

JE

Shell winding to the right, conical and pointed or rounded. 4 genera and 8 species.

251. Great pond-snail. *Limnaea stagnalis* (L.). Found mostly in ponds or slow-flowing "hard" water with abundant vegetation. Whorls stretched out lengthwise, pointed, almost as high as the opening into the shell. Last whorl convexly enlarged. Adults, 45–60 mm. long, 20–30 mm. wide. Shell fragile and pale, horn-coloured. Southern and central England, but rare in the north.

252. Marsh snail. *Limnaea palustris* (Müller). Found in standing and slow-flowing soft water, ditches and marshes, and in brackish and salt water. 6 regular whorls, increasing regularly in size. Seams not deep. Last whorl not convexly enlarged. Surface often wrinkled. Length, 20–36 mm.; width, 11–18 mm. Horny yellow to brown.

253. Dwarf pond-snail. *Limnaea* (*Galba*) *truncatula* (Müller). Found in small areas of soft water, springs, pools and ditches. Can spend long periods of drought buried in mud. Also sits at the edge of the water on plants, stones, etc. Host for larvae of the liver fluke (*Fasciola hepatica*). As 252, but shell with 5–6 domed whorls set like steps. Length, up to 10 mm.; width, about 5 mm. Horny yellow.

254. Mud snail. *Limnaea glabra* (Müller). Not common, confined to marshes, ditches and ponds which dry up. Can survive periods of drought buried in the mud. Opening of shell only one-third as long as length of shell. Length, about 14 mm.; width, 4·5 mm. Dark horny yellow.

255. Ear pond-snail. *Limnaea* (*Radix*) *auricularia* (L.). Normally found in standing water with many plants; fairly common. Whorls pointed, always shorter than the opening. Last whorl large, markedly ear-shaped in opening. Height, 25–30 mm.; width, 20–30 mm.

255a. Limnaea (*Radix*) *auricularia* (L.). From the side of opening into shell.

256. Limnaea (*Radix*) *ovata* (L.). From side of opening. Form of shell varied, normally oval. Taller than it is wide. Whorls short and cone-shaped, mouth opening oval and wide. Height, 20 mm.; width, 15 mm. Now considered to be a form of *L. pereger*, No. 257.

257. Wandering snail. *Limnaea* (*Radix*) *pereger* (Müller). Found in ponds, lakes and slow-flowing rivers. In both hard and soft water. The commonest and most abundant species. Last whorl not inflated and compressed somewhat to the side. Height, 15–20 mm.; width, 12 mm.

258. Glutinous snail. *Myxas glutinosa* (Müller). Found in still water with abundant vegetation; rare. Shell very thin, yellowish, transparent, smooth and gleaming. Mantle yellow-brown with black mottling. Can almost entirely cloak the shell. Height, 10–15 mm.; width, 8–11 mm.

258a. Myxas glutinosa (Müller) seen from the aperture.

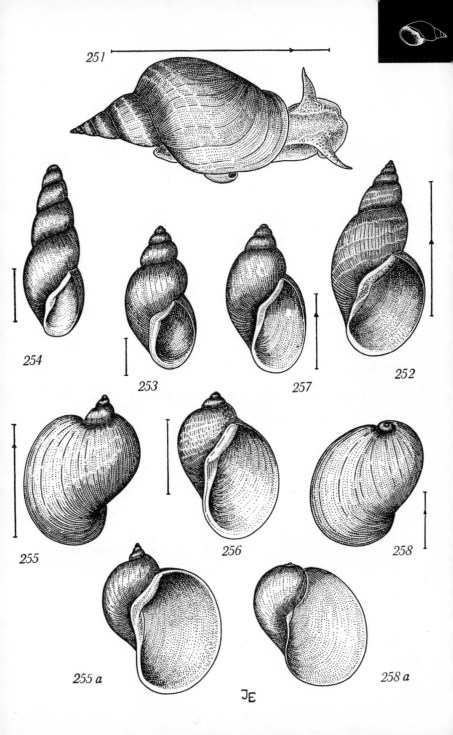

251

254

253

257

252

255

256

258

255 a

258 a

JE

TRUMPET SNAILS (*Planorbidae*). Shell winding to the left and coiled in a flat spiral.

259. Great ramshorn. *Planorbis corneus* (L.). Fairly common in lakes. 5½ whorls, rapidly widening, completely round. Shell, olive to brown. Height, 12 mm.; diameter, about 30 mm.

260. Ramshorn. *Planorbis planorbis* (L.). Underside. Common, often found in small ponds. 5–6 whorls, slowly widening, upper side markedly domed, underneath less domed. It has a string-shaped keel near the underside (260*a*). Yellow to horny brown, shining. Height, 4 mm.; diameter, 12–20 mm.

Keeled ramshorn. *Planorbis carinatus* Müller. Common in large ponds, also in algae beds of clear lakes. 4–5 whorls, rapidly widening, equally domed on both sides. Keel situated in the middle of the whorls (260*b*). Yellowish-grey. Height, 2–3 mm.; diameter, 14–17 mm.

261. Whirlpool ramshorn. *Planorbis* (*Spiralina*) *vortex* (L.). Common; typically found in running water with vegetation, but sometimes in ponds. Shell has thin wall, flat and disc-like, underneath completely even. 6–7 whorls, widening slowly, the last almost twice as wide as the penultimate, domed on top, flat underneath. Keel sharp, but not set out like a thread, close to the underside (261*a*). Joints underneath like threads and above deeply indented. Dirty yellow. Height, 1–1·5 mm.; diameter, 9–10 mm.

262. Button ramshorn. *Planorbis* (*Anisus*) *spirorbis* (L.). Widely distributed in shallow, overgrown ditches with clear water but not in mountainous areas. 5–5½ whorls, rounded, both sides domed, obtuse edge near the underside greyish-yellow. Height, about 1·7 mm.; diameter, 5–7 mm. For view of shell aperture, see 262*a*.

263. Nautilus ramshorn. *Planorbis* (*Armiger*) *crista* (L.). Widely distributed in ponds and marshes. In its typical form, ribbed and almost flat on top; underneath forming wide umbilicus. 3½–4 whorls. Greyish-white to dark horn colour. Height, 0·5–1 mm.; diameter, up to 3 mm. For view of shell aperture, see 263*a*.

264. Smooth ramshorn. *Planorbis* (*Gyraulus*) *laevis* Alder. Not very common; found in north England and Scotland among plants in lakes. Indented in the middle on top, underneath convex like a dish. 4½–5 whorls round without a keel, the last whorl somewhat widened towards the opening. Joints deep, smooth, shining, yellowish-horn-coloured. Height, 1–1·5 mm.; diameter, 5–6 mm. For view of shell aperture, see 264*a*.

265. Twisted ramshorn. *Planorbis* (*Bathyiomphalus*) *contortus* (L.). Seen from above. Widespread in large lakes. 7–8 whorls, much higher than it is wide, very tightly rolled like a strap. On top lying in one plane, underneath forming a wide cone-shaped umbilicus. Joints deep. Brown. Height, 1·75–2 mm.; diameter 5–6 mm. Underneath shown in 265*a* and shell aperture in 265*b*.

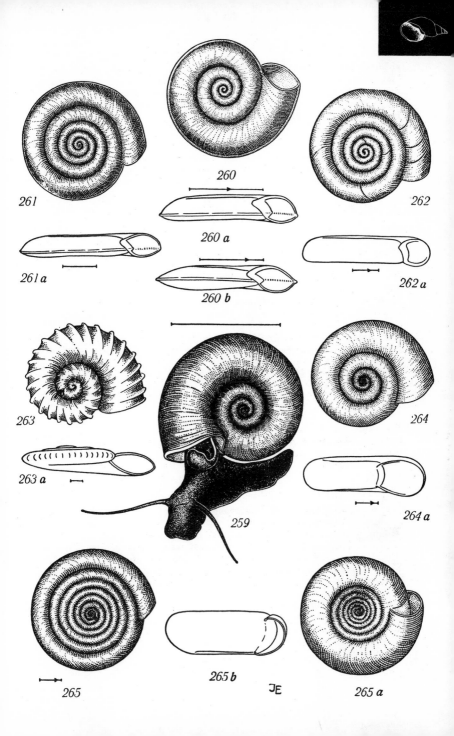

261

260

260 a

261 a

260 b

262

262 a

263

263 a

259

264

264 a

265

265 b

JE

265 a

266. River snail. *Viviparus viviparus* (L.). ♂. Greenish-brown with three dark bands. Height, 30–40 mm.; width, 24–30 mm. A very similar species, *V. fasciatus*, shell slimmer, whorls not set in steps. Common in south England, but not found north of Yorkshire.

Hydrobiidae

267. Jenkins' spire shell. *Potamopyrgus* (*Hydrobia*) *jenkinsi* Smith. 5½ whorls; shell somewhat thick; the last whorl large. Body pale-grey; shell dark-brown or black. Height, up to 5 mm.; width, 3 mm. Common in running water of all kinds; rarely in closed ponds. This species has invaded fresh water from brackish water in the last seventy years.

268. *Bithynia tentaculata* (L.). Common in lakes though rarely in ponds, as far as the alga reaches, to a depth of several metres. Feeds on detritus. Sexes separate. Shell, 5–6 whorls, slightly domed. Joints fairly deep. Horn-yellow to reddish. Height, 10–12 mm.; width, 6–7 mm.

269. *Lartetia* sp. Only found in cave and spring water with lime content. Shell yellowish to white, transparent and shining. Height, to 5 mm.; width, to about 2 mm., usually smaller. Central Europe; not found in Britain.

270. *Amnicola* (*Bythinella*) *dunkeri* Frfld. In springs and streams from springs. 4–5 whorls, the last 2 much larger than the previous ones, shell aperture having an obtuse angle on top, taking up most of two-fifths of the height. Greenish. Height, 2·5 mm.; width, 1·5 mm. Central Europe; not found in Britain.

VALVE SNAILS (*Valvatidae*)

271. Valve snail. *Valvata piscinalis* (Müller). Common in running water, but seldom in closed ponds. Greenish or yellowish, shiny. Height, 5 mm.; width, 5 mm. Shell aperture and operculum almost circular, as in the case of other species of the genus.

BLADDER SNAILS (*Physidae*). Shell winding to the left.

272. Fountain bladder snail. *Physa fontinalis* (L.). Common in clear running water with abundant vegetation. Very active. Mantle with black spots. Tentacles long and pointed. Eyes on their inner base. Edge of mantle drawn out in finger-like processes, which reflex over the shell and can almost cover it. Very wide aperture. Foot long and thin. Shell very thin, horn-coloured, smooth, shiny and transparent. 3–4 whorls, the last one being much inflated. Height, 10–11 mm.; width, 6–8 mm.

273. Moss bladder snail. *Aplecta hypnorum* (L.). Found in ditches and ponds, chiefly on moors. Animal blackish-blue, tentacles long and awl-shaped. Mantle has whole edge, grey, black spots. Shell smooth, shiny, brownish and transparent. 6 whorls, the last not being inflated. Height, 12–15 mm.; width, 5 mm.

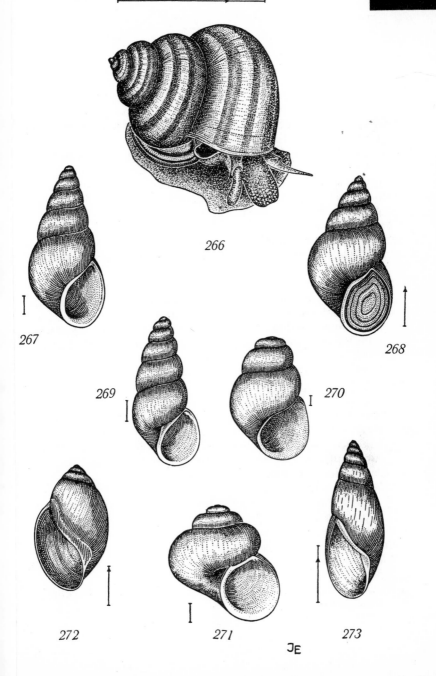

266

267

268

269

270

272

271

273

JE

Glossary

Amoebocyte. A blood cell of no constant shape; resembling the protozoan *Amoeba.*

Antenna. Paired appendage on the head of insects and Crustacea, usually long, many-jointed and mobile. Used as an organ of touch, smell, etc.

Axil. Angle between the upper side of a leaf and the stem that it grows from; normal position for lateral buds.

Bract. Small leaf, in the axil of which a flower develops.

Calcareous. Containing lime, limestone or chalk.

Calyx. Outermost part of a flower, consisting of green, leaf-like sepals.

Campodeid, campodeiform. Resembling the wingless insect, *Campodea*, having an elongated, well-sclerotised body, jaws pointing forwards, long legs, and usually a pair of cerci at the tail.

Carpel. Female part of a flower, consisting of the ovary, which contains the seeds, and the stigma, which receives the pollen grains.

Cephalothorax. The united segments of the head and thorax of higher Crustacea (Decapoda).

Cerci. Paired appendages at the hind end of the abdomen of many insects.

Chitin. Tough, resistant outer covering layer of insects and Crustacea, composed of a nitrogen-containing polysaccharide.

Cilia. Microscopic, short, hair-like threads which project from the surface of a cell or organism. The cilia beat back and forth, as flagella do, and set up small water currents.

Ciliated. Covered with cilia.

Corolla. The coloured part of a flower inside the calyx, consisting of a group of petals.

Coxa. Basal (first) segment of the insect leg.

Crenate. Having the edge (of a leaf) notched with rounded teeth.

Dioecious. Having unisexual (male and female) flowers on separate plants.

Distal. Situated away from the centre of the body or the point of attachment.

Dystrophic. Describes conditions occurring in freshwater bog pools and mountain lakes where the water contains much humus and undecomposed plant material, little dissolved oxygen and is very acid in reaction.

Elytron (pl. *elytra*). Modified front wing of beetles, which is thick, tough and acts as a wing-case for the thin, folded hind wing beneath it.

Ensiform. Sword-shaped.

Epithelium. Sheet of firmly coherent cells that lines cavities and tubes or exposed surfaces of the body. It often contains glands.

Eruciform. Like a caterpillar in appearance.

Eutrophic. Describes conditions of a lake which has a shallow shore zone with abundant vegetation, water that is rich in dissolved nutrient salts and is slightly alkaline in reaction. Typical of ponds, marshes and wet meadows.

Femur. Of insects, one of the segments (third from base) of the leg.

Flagellum. A fine, long thread (projecting from a cell of an organism) which beats back and forth with a characteristically S-shaped movement.

Funiculus. A short stalk, usually supporting the ovary of a flower.

Gemmule. Organ of vegetative (asexual) reproduction in mosses and liverworts.

Glume. Bract, pair of which occur at the base of a spikelet in the flower of a grass (family Gramineae).

Hermaphrodite (*bisexual*). Of a flower, having both stamens and carpels in the same flower. Of an animal, producing both eggs and sperm.

Hydrosere. The succession of communities of animals and plants which occur in an enclosed lake as it gradually fills in by accumulation of silt and plant debris.

Labium. Lower lip of insect.

Lamella. Thin wafer or plate-like structure.

Larva. The pre-adult form, in which many invertebrate animals hatch from the egg; capable of fending for itself, though usually in a way different from the adult. Usually incapable of sexual reproduction and often very different from the mature adult in shape and form.

Mandibles. Of insects and Crustacea, first pair of mouth-parts, which usually do the work of biting and crushing food.

Maxillae. Of insects and Crustacea, second pair of mouth-parts, lying behind the mandibles; assist in eating.

Mesothorax. The second segment of an insect's thorax, bearing a pair of wings or wing cases and the second pair of legs.

Metathorax. The third and last segment of an insect's thorax, bearing the hind pair of wings.

Monoecious. Of plants, having unisexual (male and female) flowers on the same plant. Of animals, hermaphrodite.

Nymph. Young stage of heterometabolous insects (e.g. may-flies and dragon-flies) which resembles the adult in having the same general body form, mouth-parts and compound eyes. Differing in being sexually immature and with only partially developed wings. The term is now going into disuse, as *larva* is used to define immature pre-adult stages of all insects.

Oligotrophic. Describes condition of lakes that are poor in food materials, usually with a steep shoreline and little marginal vegetation, often with water with an acid reaction.

Osculum. An opening in the body of sponges through which water is discharged.

Ovary. The female reproductive organ, in which the (animal) eggs or (plant) seeds are contained.

Palmate. Of a leaf with more than three leaflets arising from the same point.

Palp. A jointed, finger-like appendage on the mouth-parts of insects and Crustacea; used in tasting food or assisting eating.

Panicle. Branched conical inflorescence.

Papilla. A projection from the surface of the skin.

Parapodium. Paired paddle-like appendage extending from the sides of some Annelid worms; a pseudopod, q.v.; abdominal false foot.

Perianth. The outer part of a flower, enclosing the stamens and carpels. Composed of sepals and petals.

Petiole. Leaf-stalk.

Photosynthesis. Synthesis by green plants of carbohydrate foodstuffs from water and carbon dioxide with the aid of energy absorbed from sunlight.

Pinnate. Leaf composed of more than three leaflets arranged in two rows along the stalk.

Plankton. Floating or drifting animals and plants of the sea or a lake. Mostly very small and occurring near the water surface.

Polyp. Sedentary form of a Coelenterate, e.g. *Hydra.* Cylindrical trunk fixed at one end, with a single mouth aperture surrounded by a ring of tentacles at the other.

Proleg. Stumpy appendage with no joints on the abdomen of caterpillars.

Prothorax. The first segment of an insect's thorax, bearing the first
pair of legs but no wings.

Proximal. Situated close to the place of attachment.

Pseudopod. A soft, foot-like abdominal appendage, characteristic of
the larvae of many flies (Diptera); a parapodium, q.v.

Pupa. Stage between larva and adult of insects, in which locomotion
and feeding cease, but great developmental changes occur. In
butterflies, known as a chrysalis.

Raceme. Unbranched conical inflorescence in which the flowers are
borne on small stalks.

Rhabdite. Minute, rod-shaped bodies in the skin of flatworms. They
may be discharged in the water and are possibly used in defence.

Rhizome. Underground stem of plant, lasting for more than one
growing season and often acting as a food-store.

Rostrum. A snout-like prolongation of the head, especially in bugs
and some beetles (e.g. weevils).

Scape. Upright, leafless flowering stem of a plant, all of whose
foliage leaves grow straight from the root.

Sclerotin. Fibrous, insoluble protein responsible for the dark, hard
qualities of insect cuticle.

Sclerotised. Hardened and darkened by the deposition of sclerotin,
a fibrous protein which forms the hard parts of insects.

Serrate. Toothed like a saw.

Siliceous. Containing silica.

Spadix. An inflorescence in the form of a spike with a thick fleshy
axis, e.g. cuckoo pint, arum lily.

Spathulate. Paddle-shaped.

Sporocarp. Spore-producing organ of liverworts and mosses.

Sporophyll. Leaf of a fern that bears spore-producing organs.

Stamen. Male organ of flower that produces pollen.

Statoblast. Resistant reproductive body produced by freshwater
Polyzoa.

Stigma. Tip of stalked portion of ovary that receives pollen grains.

Stipule. Small leaf-like appendage formed one on either side of a
leaf stalk, protecting axillary buds.

Symbiosis. A permanent association of two dissimilar organisms
that is often advantageous to both of them.

Tarsus. The last main segment of the insect leg, made up of a variable number of joints (tarsal segments, or tarsi).

Thallus. Plant body of liverworts, mosses and algae, showing no true differentiation into root, stem or leaf, as in higher plants.

Tibia. One of the segments (fourth from base) of an insect leg.

Trachea. Air-filled breathing tube of insects, many of which branch through the body from a few openings (spiracles) at the surface.

Turion. A detached winter-bud by which many water-plants spend the winter.

Umbel. An umbrella-shaped inflorescence.

Bibliography

Detailed references for identification of specific groups of animals are given at the end of each section throughout this book. More general works on freshwater life and methods for field-work are given below.

Clegg, J. (1965). *The Freshwater Life of the British Isles.* 3rd edition. Wayside and Woodland series. Warne. London.

Dowdeswell, W. H. (1959). *Practical Animal Ecology.* Methuen, London.

Imms, A. D. (1947). *Insect Natural History.* New Naturalist Series, No. 8. Collins, London.

Macan, T. T. (1963) *Freshwater Ecology.* Longmans, London.

Macan, T. T. (1959). *A Guide to Freshwater Invertebrate Animals.* Longmans, London.

Macan, T. T. (1970). *Biological Studies of the English Lakes.* Longmans. London.

Macan, T. T., and Worthington, E. B. (1951). *Life in Lakes and Rivers.* New Naturalist Series, No. 15, and revised edition (1972). Fontana New Naturalist series. Collins. London.

Mellanby, H. (1963). *Animal Life in Fresh Water.* 6th edition. Methuen, London.

Sankey, J. (1958). *A Guide to Field Biology.* Longmans, London.

Ward, H. B., and Whipple, G. C. *Freshwater Biology.* 2nd edition (1959). Editor: W. T. Edmondson. Wiley, New York.

Index

204